Introduct

The beautiful **Llangollen Canal** rur
at Horseshoe Falls across the border
visiting the historic towns of Llang
Whitchurch, as well as ancient villages. It ‗ ‗ ‗ ‗ ‗‗‗‗‗‗‗‗₀
Vale of Llangollen, enclosed by hills and now part of a designated Area of
Outstanding Natural Beauty, then crosses north Shropshire, with its glacial
meres and rare raised mosses, to the junction with the main Shropshire
Union Canal in south Cheshire. The narrow canal was designed by William
Jessop and Thomas Telford, the greatest civil engineers of that era. Its most
spectacular 11 mile section from Horseshoe Falls to bridge 19 at Chirk Bank,
featuring two stunning aqueducts and tunnels, was awarded World Heritage
Site status in 2009. Its centerpiece is Telford's Pontcysyllte Aqueduct,
described as a 'masterpiece of creative genius'.

The canal was originally part of the Ellesmere Canal, an ambitious scheme
launched in 1793, to create a commercial waterway linking the river Mersey,
from what became Ellesmere Port, to the river Dee at Chester and the river
Severn at Shrewsbury. Its aim was to serve the mineral industries of north
east Wales, West Midlands manufacturing centres, and distribute lime as a
fertiliser to enrich farmland in Shropshire. By 1805 only part of the canal
system had been completed and the plan to extend south from Chester to
Trevor was abandoned, as was the final nine miles into Shrewsbury.

A new feeder source was needed so the canal was extended to the Dee
near Llangollen in 1808. It was also decided to join the canal with the Chester
Canal at Hurleston. In 1845 it became part of the wider Shropshire Union
Canal system.

Goods carried included coal, iron, limestone, lime, timber, grain, and
cheese. Traffic peaked in the mid-19thC, but had ceased by the late 1930s.
The canal survived formal closure in 1944 mainly because it fed water to
Hurleston reservoir. It was later renamed the Llangollen Canal and is now
one of the most popular canals in Britain, with an estimated 15,000 boat trips
along it each year. Ironic really, since Llangollen was not included in the
original plans!

This book comprehensively explores the canal, its history and the
adjoining countryside, visiting places of interest. It contains 29 circular
walks plus 9 linear walks linked to local buses and a heritage railway. Three
walks feature the connecting restored section of the scenic Montgomery
Canal. Many feature canalside or country pubs, and tea-rooms (check
opening times). The routes range from a 1¾ mile stroll around Cole Mere
in Shropshire to a 11 mile linear World Heritage Site walk. A key feature is
that routes can easily be linked with others to provide longer day walks, if
required.

Please observe The Country Code. Enjoy your walking!

WALK I

HORSESHOE FALLS

DESCRIPTION A 4¾ mile walk featuring delightful valley, canal and river scenery, and the historic town of Llangollen. The route first visits 15thC Llantisilio Church, then heads to the source of the Llangollen Canal at the famous Horseshoe Falls by the river Dee. It then follows the canal to the Chainbridge Hotel and crosses the restored historic Chain Bridge over the Dee to Berwyn Station. After rising from the valley, it continues across the part wooded hillside, with good views, then descends to Llangollen. It returns along the narrow scenic first section of the canal, featuring horse-drawn boats. Allow about 3 hours. It can be started from Llangollen Bridge or the International Pavilion car park.

START Llantisilio Green car park [SJ 198433]

DIRECTIONS From Llangollen take the A542 towards Ruthin, then turn left on the B5103 signposted to Corwen/Rhewl/Horseshoe Falls. After ½ mile, at a junction, keep ahead to find the car park on the left.

I From the toilets follow a path to an information board by a kissing gate, then a path across the top of the sloping field near the road to Llantisilio Church. *It contains a fine medieval roof and a rare medieval oak eagle lectern.* Follow the path down past the churchyard, through gates by the river Dee, and on past the Horseshoe Falls – *a crescent shaped weir built by Thomas Telford for diverting water into the Llangollen Canal* – to a gate by the Meter House. *It measures the amount of water, about 12 million gallons a day, extracted from the Dee to supply the canal and south Cheshire with drinking water.* Continue along the narrow shallow feeder canal, under a road bridge, and past the rear of the Chain Bridge Hotel, dating from 1828. *At its entrance is an information board on the nearby Chain Bridge.*

2 Go past the front of the hotel to cross the Chain Bridge over the river. Follow the zig zag path up to pass under the railway line to the A5 by Berwyn Station. Turn LEFT along the pavement, then cross with care to a short rising enclosed path opposite, by the nearby side road and house, to the road. Follow it RIGHT past cottages and up beneath woodland. At Tan y Bedw Ucha's garage do a U-turn LEFT to follow a signposted path back across the wooded slope, rising gently to eventually reach the bend of a stony

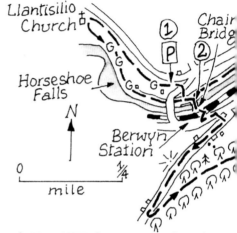

track. Turn LEFT down it – *shortly with a view of Eglwyseg limestone escarpment and Castell Dinas Bran.*

3 At a lane end turn RIGHT up the access track to pass Hillside Cottage. Go down a path to a stile and on to another, then follow the undulating path through Inman's Wood to a stile. After crossing a bracken covered slope the path continues beside a fence across the steep wooded slope to a stile, then through trees to Glas Aber. Go past the house, bend left past the garage, then right for a few yards along its access track. Steps on the left mark the start of a tree-lined sunken path, which may be hidden by undergrowth in summer. Follow the improving path past a section of iron fence, then the side of Bryn Awel to a narrow road. Follow it down beneath woodland to the A5 in Llangollen. Cross to the pavement opposite and follow it LEFT above Riverside Park to a gate at its corner. Go down a tree-lined pathway then turn RIGHT along Victoria Promenade above the river. Later, take the left fork to join a narrow road at The Corn Mill. Follow it ahead to the town's main street.

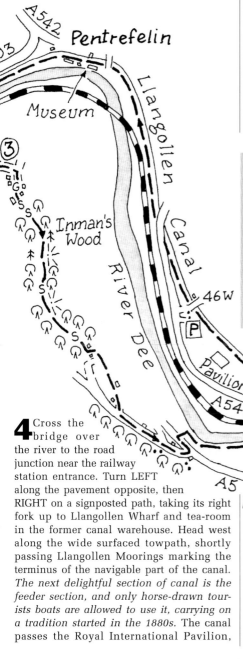

which hosts the world famous International Musical Eisteddfod each July, the sidings of the Llangollen Railway, then the Motor Museum at Pentrefelin – *from the mid 19thC the site of a slab and slate works linked by a tramway from quarries up at Horseshoe Pass.* After bridge 48AW continue along the canalside driveway above a section of the river Dee popular with canoeists, to cross the iron footbridge over the canal at the rear of The Chain Bridge Hotel. Follow the railed stepped path up to the B5103 and turn RIGHT, then LEFT on a signposted path into the car park.

WALK 2

CHAIN BRIDGE

DESCRIPTION A delightful 2½ mile linear walk combining a short trip on a Llangollen Railway steam train with a crossing of the historic Chain Bridge, visits to Horseshoe Falls and 5thC Llantisilio Church, then a return along the popular first section of the canal, full of interest. Allow about 1½ hours.
START Berwyn Station [SJ 199432].

Take the train from Llangollen to Berwyn Station. From the eastern end of the platform take a path under the railway line and down to cross the Chain Bridge over the river Dee to the hotel and join the canal beyond. Follow it LEFT then cross the iron footbridge over the canal. At the road turn RIGHT, then LEFT on a signposted path through trees to a car park. Now follow instructions in paragraph 1 of Walk 1 and paragraph 2 of the main route in Walk 3 to Llangollen Wharf. Afterwards follow a path down to the A5 by the station entrance and Llangollen Bridge.

4 Cross the bridge over the river to the road junction near the railway station entrance. Turn LEFT along the pavement opposite, then RIGHT on a signposted path, taking its right fork up to Llangollen Wharf and tea-room in the former canal warehouse. Head west along the wide surfaced towpath, shortly passing Llangollen Moorings marking the terminus of the navigable part of the canal. *The next delightful section of canal is the feeder section, and only horse-drawn tourists boats are allowed to use it, carrying on a tradition started in the 1880s.* The canal passes the Royal International Pavilion,

3

WALK 3

VALLE CRUCIS ABBEY

DESCRIPTION A stunning 6 mile walk (**A**) featuring several important historic landmarks, including Valle Crucis Abbey, the finest medieval site in North Wales, and two tea-rooms. The route, waymarked as Llangollen History Trail, first visits 15thC Llantisilio church, passes the Horseshoe Falls and the restored Chain Bridge over the river Dee, then follows the first section of the canal to Llangollen Wharf, with its tea-room. It then rises to the lower slopes of Castell Dinas Bran, with an option to climb it, adding an extra 1 mile to the walk. It continues into the beautiful Eglwyseg Valley to the 13thC Abbey ruins and nearby tea-room, then returns across the lower slopes of National Trust owned Coed Hyrddyn. Allow about 3½ hours. A shorter 2½ mile walk (**B**) is included. The walk can also start from Llangollen or from the car park by the Royal International Pavilion, from where the nearby canal can be joined at bridge 46W.
START Llantisilio Green car park [SJ 198433]
DIRECTIONS See Walk 1

1 Follow instructions in paragraph 1 of Walk 1.

2 Continue along the hotel's canalside access road above the river – *whose rapids are popular with canoeists. Only horse-drawn tourists boats are allowed to use this delightful feeder section of canal to the mooring basin, carrying on a tradition started in the 1880s.* From bridge 48AW continue along the canal, shortly passing through Pentrefelin – *from the mid 19thC the site of a slab and slate works by a canal wharf, linked by a tramway from quarries up at Horseshoe Pass, now a Motor museum.* (For **Walk B** cross over bridge 48W to the A542. Turn right up the pavement. After about 50 yards cross with care to a stony track opposite beneath a house to join a signposted path to Valle Crucis Abbey. Go through the gate and follow the stony track past farm buildings. After two gates, where the track bends

left through a gate turn right along a narrower track to a small gate just before its end at point 5.) Continue along the canal past the sidings of the Llangollen Railway, the Royal International Pavilion, which hosts the world famous International Musical Eisteddfod each July, then a mooring basin marking the terminus of the navigable part of the canal. Soon afterwards you reach Llangollen Wharf and tea-room in a former warehouse.

3 Cross the road bridge over the canal and at the junction go up steps ahead and follow the signposted enclosed path up past a school and beside a field – *enjoying a view of Castell Dinas Bran* – to a kissing gate onto an access lane. Follow the path ahead up to another kissing gate above a house. Go up its access track to a junction of tracks and lane. Go up the narrow stony track ahead to a kissing

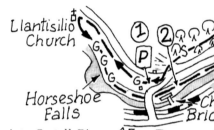

gate into Castell Dinas Bran site. (For Castell Dinas Bran take the right fork.) Take the signposted Llangollen History Trail path ahead to a wooden bird sculpture waymark post. Take the path's left fork down beside the fence to cross a stile. Go down the field edge – *with a view of 18thC Dinbren Hall.* At the corner turn LEFT along the bottom field edge to a stile/gate. Turn RIGHT up the road past woodland, a verge managed as a roadside nature reserve, then Dinbren Lodge to a junction. Turn RIGHT along Dinbren Road.

4 On the bend by Caledfryn cottage take the signposted path on the left along Bryn Hyfryd's access track, then behind the cottage to a stile/gate. Follow the wide path to a gate. The delightful path briefly descends then continues across the steep part wooded hillside – *with a view across*

4

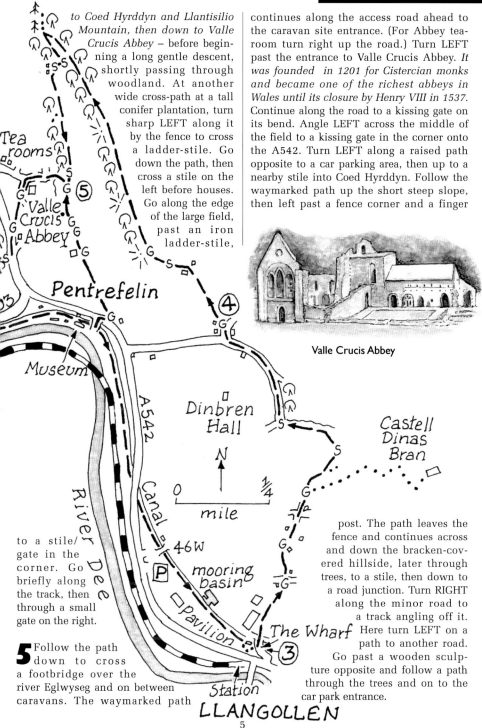

to Coed Hyrddyn and Llantisilio Mountain, then down to Valle Crucis Abbey – before beginning a long gentle descent, shortly passing through woodland. At another wide cross-path at a tall conifer plantation, turn sharp LEFT along it by the fence to cross a ladder-stile. Go down the path, then cross a stile on the left before houses. Go along the edge of the large field, past an iron ladder-stile,

continues along the access road ahead to the caravan site entrance. (For Abbey tea-room turn right up the road.) Turn LEFT past the entrance to Valle Crucis Abbey. *It was founded in 1201 for Cistercian monks and became one of the richest abbeys in Wales until its closure by Henry VIII in 1537.* Continue along the road to a kissing gate on its bend. Angle LEFT across the middle of the field to a kissing gate in the corner onto the A542. Turn LEFT along a raised path opposite to a car parking area, then up to a nearby stile into Coed Hyrddyn. Follow the waymarked path up the short steep slope, then left past a fence corner and a finger

Valle Crucis Abbey

Tea rooms

Valle Crucis Abbey

Pentrefelin

④

Museum

A542

Dinbren Hall

N

0   ¼   mile

Castell Dinas Bran

River Dee

Canal

46W

P

mooring basin

Pavilion

The Wharf

③

Station

LLANGOLLEN

to a stile/ gate in the corner. Go briefly along the track, then through a small gate on the right.

5 Follow the path down to cross a footbridge over the river Eglwyseg and on between caravans. The waymarked path

post. The path leaves the fence and continues across and down the bracken-covered hillside, later through trees, to a stile, then down to a road junction. Turn RIGHT along the minor road to a track angling off it. Here turn LEFT on a path to another road. Go past a wooden sculpture opposite and follow a path through the trees and on to the car park entrance.

CASTELL DINAS BRAN

DESCRIPTION An undulating 5 mile walk featuring a scenic section of canal, a country pub mid-way, and a spectacular hilltop medieval castle ruin above Llangollen offering superb views. The route follows a scenic part wooded narrow section of the canal eastwards to the Sun Trevor pub, then follows a narrow scenic road across mid-slopes overlooking the Vale of Llangollen and up to another road beneath impressive Trevor Rocks. It then climbs to Castell Dinas Bran (1,000 feet/320 metres), before descending to Llangollen. Allow about 3 hours.

START Llangollen Bridge [SJ 215422].

DIRECTIONS The ancient stone road bridge over the river Dee lies at the northern end of the town's main street.

Llangollen, which gets its name from St Collen, who established a church here in the 6thC developed around a natural crossing point of the river Dee. The present Llangollen Bridge – one of the Seven Wonders of Wales – is attributed to Dr John Trevor, Bishop of St Asaph and dates to 1345. An additional arch was added in 1861 to accommodate the railway and the bridge was later widened. During the 19thC textile mills developed nearby beside the Dee, the last one closing in 1967. It was an important staging post on the London-Holyhead coach route and has been a mecca for tourists and eminent travellers since the late 18thC.

Castell Dinas Bran, now a romantic ruin, with many legends associated with it, occupies a prime strategic position on the site of an Iron Age fort on top of a steep isolated hill overlooking the town. The castle is believed to have been built about 1260 by the Welsh Prince, Gruffydd ap Madoc. By 1277 it had been deliberately abandoned and burned to prevent its use by Edward I's invading army. An English garrison was placed there, and despite its subsequent return to Welsh ownership, the castle was never rebuilt.

I Cross the bridge over the river to the road junction near the entrance to Llangollen Station. Turn LEFT along the pavement opposite, then RIGHT on a signposted path, taking its right fork up to The Wharf tearoom in the former canal warehouse. Go under nearby bridge 45 and follow the picturesque narrow canal eastwards – *with a view up to Castell Dinas Bran* – for 1¼ miles. Just before bridge 41W go through a kissing gate and up to cross the bridge to the adjoining A539. Go up the road opposite to the Sun Trevor. Just beyond do a sharp U-turn LEFT to the entrance to Haulfryn and go up the narrow enclosed path, turning left at a junction and rising more steeply to Tan y bont. Turn LEFT up the nearby road and over a cattle grid.

2 Continue along the scenic upland road, later rising to a junction. Turn LEFT along the road beneath the limestone scree-covered slopes of Trevor Rocks towards Castell Dinas Bran. Shortly turn LEFT over a cattle grid along a side road to a kissing gate. Follow the waymarked path up the hillside to a small gate and up to the castle ruins. Go across its top, then follow a zig-zag path down its western slope. Continue up and across a wide grassy area, then down a short stony path to a kissing gate. Descend the nearby house's narrow stony access track to a junction of stony tracks and a lane.

3 Go along the narrow stony track signposted to Llangollen, down past Bryn Castell to a kissing gate above a house. Follow the path down the field edge and over a lane to a kissing gate. Go down the enclosed path past a school to a road junction. Follow the road over the canal by The Wharf and down to the road to Riverside Taxidermy and nearby Llangollen Bridge.

WALK 5

LLANDYN HALL

DESCRIPTION A 4½ mile waymarked Community Miles walk. It follows Walk 4 along the canal to the Sun Trevor pub then returns on good paths across the attractive mid-slopes overlooking the Vale of Llangollen past Llandyn Hall. Allow about 3 hours.

START As Walk 4.

1 Follow instructions in paragraph 1 of Walk 4.

2 Just beyond the cattle grid angle LEFT on the signposted path down to a stile/gate. Turn RIGHT down the path past trees, behind a large garden wall and cottage, then through an old tree boundary to a waymark post. Turn LEFT down the field to a finger post/ stile. Go across the next field to a stile into a small dingle. Follow the path across a large footbridge over a stream. Soon turn RIGHT up an enclosed path to a gate and a stony track to a house. Go up its access lane past an old cottage. On its bend cross a stile on the left. Follow the waymarked path across the mid-slopes of the large field to gates at its far fence corner. Go down the green track to further gates near outbuildings of Llandyn Hall, then down to a stile/gate. *The large barn nearby dates from the late 17thC.* Cross a nearby stile on the Hall's driveway and go up the field to gates in its corner. The waymarked path rises with the fence, at its corner bending left up to a small gate/stile. Cross a stile just beyond and go half-LEFT up the field to an old gateway, then up the next field edge past Wern-uchaf to a stile onto a narrow road. Go briefly along the road and through a waymarked gate ahead, then along a green track past a small ruin. Now follow a path along the edge of two fields, then an enclosed path past dwellings, including Geufron Hall, to a junction of stony tracks and a lane. Turn LEFT.

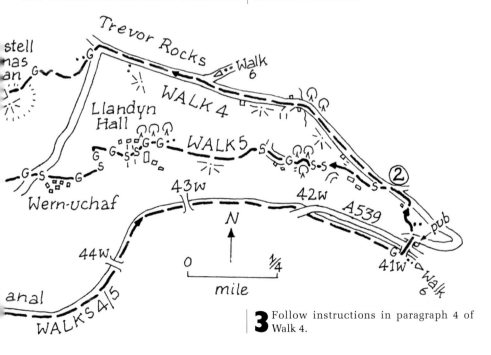

3 Follow instructions in paragraph 4 of Walk 4.

WALK 6
PANORAMA WALK

DESCRIPTION A delightful 6 mile walk exploring the northern side of the Vale of Llangollen, with a pub midway and at the end. The route follows the Offa's Dyke Path (ODP) across the wooded slopes up to a scenic upland road, known as the Panorama Walk, which it follows beneath impressive limestone escarpments, enjoying extensive views. It then descends another scenic road and path to the Sun Trevor pub, before returning along the canal. Allow about 3 hours.
START Trevor Basin [SJ 272423].
DIRECTIONS From Llangollen, take the A539 towards Wrexham. At Trevor, turn right down the B5434 signposted to Froncysyllte and Pontcysyllte World Heritage Site, then left into New Road. Go over the bridge to enter a car park on your right, alongside Trevor Basin.

In Trevor Basin cross the footbridge over the canal and go through the car park to a road. Turn LEFT, then RIGHT along a signposted path beside the canal and over footbridge 32W. Go down the ramp and along the towpath. Soon follow the ODP across footbridge 33W then up the field to a kissing gate by the former Ruabon – Barmouth railway embankment. The path passes under the old line and continues to the A539 at Trevor. Cross the road with care and turn LEFT along the pavement. Shortly, turn RIGHT along Trevor Hall Road. On a bend by Gardener's Lodge, follow the ODP along Trevor Hall's stony access track ahead, then through a kissing gate on the right. The ODP rises through trees, passes a field, then continues through Trevor Hall Wood.

2 At a signposted path junction, follow the ODP down through conifers then at the next junction along the right fork through woodland, passing above a house. The ODP continues through mixed woodland, passes through two gates, then beneath a house and rises to a small gate. It then turns right up beside a wall and follows the house's stony access track up onto the Panorama Walk.

Continue along the narrow upland road. Later, at a junction, turn sharp LEFT along the side road heading back across the hillside, soon on a long steady descent. After Ty Nant it levels out and continues across the steep hillside. Later, it crosses a cattle grid and descends. *Hidden above the road in the former Trevor quarry are the remains of large lime kilns.*

3 Soon, turn sharp RIGHT on a signposted Community Miles Route path to nearby Tan y bont. Descend steps then follow the enclosed path down to a signposted path junction. Turn RIGHT down the path to the entrance to Haulfryn. Just beyond turn RIGHT down the road to the Sun Trevor, then go across the nearby A539 and bridge 41 over the canal. Turn RIGHT down to a kissing gate onto the towpath. Go under the bridge and follow the canal back to join your outward route – *after bridge 35W enjoying a good view of 18thC Trevor Hall.*

WALK 7
TREVOR BASIN

DESCRIPTION This 2½ mile walk takes you along sections of the former Ruabon - Barmouth railway line and the canal. Allow about 1½ hours.
START Trevor Basin [SJ 272423]. See Walk 6.

*D*uring the early 19thC, Trevor Basin, connected by tramways and a short canal to Cefn Mawr, became an important wharf serving local quarries, collieries, ironworks and brickworks. Canal traffic declined after the building of the Ruabon-Barmouth railway in the 1860s, with a station at Trevor, which transported lime from Trevor and

8

brought visitors to the area. Today Trevor Basin is a busy service point for today's narrow boat recreational traffic and for visitors to the Pontcysyllte World Heritage Site. The railway closed in the 1960s.

low a path to the road. Turn LEFT then go through a gate opposite and the Anglo Welsh car park to cross a footbridge over the canal in Trevor Basin.

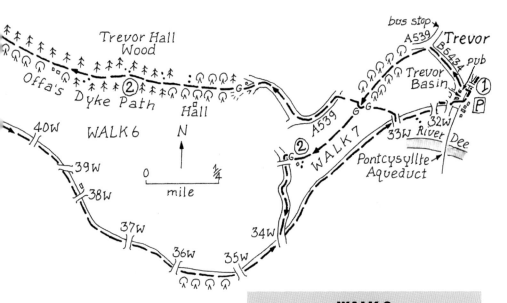

On entering Trevor Basin turn RIGHT under road bridge 29W and walk along the canal's right fork – which once extended as the Plas Kynaston canal to Cefn Mawr – then return to cross a stone stile onto the road. Turn RIGHT, then RIGHT again up Station Road to just before the A539. Go through a nearby kissing gate and follow the signposted Old Railway Line Path, shortly passing through woodland on an embankment, to a small gate. Continue through a wide cutting and along another embankment. As late as the 1950s, on Saturdays in summer, trains from different parts of England, full of passengers, many bound for Butlins in Pwllheli, passed this way.

2 At a side path and barn on the left take the waymarked path on the right down to a lane. Follow it under the railway bridge and on to cross bridge 34W over the canal. Turn LEFT down to the towpath and follow the canal back towards Trevor Basin. Later cross footbridge 32W over the canal and fol-

WALK 8

TREVOR TO LLANGOLLEN

DESCRIPTION A 4½ mile linear walk along a former railway line to join the canal heading west through the Vale of Llangollen past the Sun Trevor pub. Allow about 2 hours.
START A539/B5434 (Station Road) junction in Trevor [SJ 269425].

Take the 5 or T3 bus from Parade Street, Llangollen to the bus stop just beyond the junction in Trevor, signposted to Froncysyllte and Pontcysyllte World Heritage Site. From the top of Station Road follow instructions from the third sentence of paragraph 1 of Walk 7 along the Old Railway Path, then lane to join the canal at bridge 34W. Now follow instructions from the third sentence of paragraph 3 of Walk 9 to Llangollen.

VALE OF LLANGOLLEN

DESCRIPTION A 9 ½ mile walk around the part wooded Vale of Llangollen. The route passes through the edge of Pen-y-coed, then makes a long steady climb on a stony track/ byway across Croes yr Esgob to a great view-point at 1214 feet/ 370 metres. It continues across the hillside, then descends past a former quarry and through woodland to Froncysyllte, before following the canal across the stunning Pontcysllte Aqueduct to Trevor Basin and back to Llangollen. Allow about 5 hours.

START The War Memorial, Llangollen [SJ 215421] or Trevor Basin [SJ 272423].

DIRECTIONS The War Memorial stands on the corner of Castle Street and Bridge Street opposite The Royal. For Trevor Basin see Walk 6.

gate/gate and a road. Cross the stile opposite and follow the path through three fields to Ty-uchaf. Turn RIGHT along its access track to a waymarked gate by the house. Follow the grass path, then a stonier one through a small wood to a footbridge and a stile/gate beyond. The path continues beside the fence and rises to a path junction. Turn RIGHT along the path past a small old quarry, then by mature trees to a bridle gate and on to a road. Turn LEFT up a stony track, signposted to Pen-y-bryn, to a gate. Continue up the track – *with a good view along Pengwern Vale, once the course of the river Dee.*

2 When the track splits at a waymark post by woodland, go up its left fork. The narrow track begins a long steady climb across Croes yr Esgob – *offering extensive views* – passing through two gates. After 1 mile, as it bends to a nearby road cross a stile

Go along nearby Bridge Street then Church Street past The Hand Hotel and St Collen's church to the A5 by The Sun Inn. Turn LEFT then RIGHT up Brook Street past a car park and Horseshoe Pass View, then angle LEFT up a narrow lane, bending to a cottage and becoming a path. Just above turn RIGHT along a path signposted to Pen-y-coed to a kissing gate. The path rises past a kissing gate by Pen-y-coed and continues up across the wooded slope. Soon take its right fork to a stile and up to another stile then a kissing gate. Follow the path ahead along the bottom edge of the wood, soon by a fence. It then begins a long steady descent to a kissing

at a great viewpoint. Go across the field, shortly descending to a waymarked gate in the fence on your left. Descend a path through bracken, then turn LEFT down a road. Shortly take a signposted path behind a cottage. Follow the tree-lined stiled path across the hillside and through a small wood. It continues down a narrow ridge overlooking the former Pen-y-Graig quarry and passes houses to a road. *Limestone was moved down to the canal by a series of tramway inclines.* Turn LEFT down a nearby stony track to a stile by a large transmitter mast. Follow the waymarked path by a fence down through woodland to a stile, then an enclosed path down to a road in Froncysyllte. Turn LEFT then angle RIGHT down Methodist Hill to the A5. Cross with care to the pavement opposite by the B5434 and turn RIGHT down a side road to cross a footbridge/lift bridge over the canal. Turn LEFT along the wide towpath and across the Pontcysllte Aqueduct to Trevor Basin. *See Walks 11 & 7 for information.*

3 Cross the footbridge over the canal and go across the Anglo Welsh car park to a road. Turn LEFT then RIGHT along a path beside the canal and over footbridge 32W, then down the ramp and along the towpath. Follow the increasingly scenic canal westwards past the Sun Trevor pub, eventually passing under bridge 45W to reach Llangollen Wharf with its tea-room. Go down an initially stepped path to the main road. Turn LEFT then cross nearby Llangollen Bridge opposite.

WALK 10

FRONCYSYLLTE TO LLANGOLLEN

DESCRIPTION A 5 mile linear walk following the canal across Pontcysyllte Aqueduct to Trevor Basin, then west to Llangollen Wharf. Allow about 2 ½ hours.
START A5/B5434 junction in Froncysyllte [SJ 271412].

Take the GHA 64 bus from the end of Parade Street, Llangollen to the bus stop just beyond the Aqueduct Inn in Froncysyllte. Cross the nearby B5434 and go down the side road to cross the footbridge/ lift bridge over the canal. Follow it left to cross the Pontcysllte Aqueduct into Trevor Basin. Now follow instructions in paragraph 3 of Walk 9 back to Llangollen.

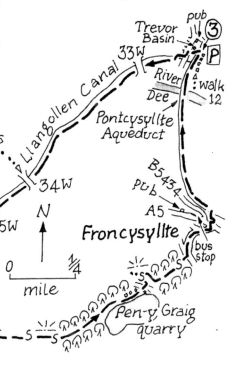

WALK 11

PONTCYSYLLTE AQUEDUCT

DESCRIPTION A 1¾ mile (A) or 1⅓ mile (B) walk featuring an exhilarating walk across the famous aqueduct. Both walks first cross the aqueduct then the canal at Froncysyllte. Walk A returns by the 17thC Dee road bridge, offering a good view of the aqueduct towering above the river, whilst Walk B returns along the western side of the canal and another crossing of the aqueduct. Allow about 1 hour. The aqueduct crossing is not suitable for those with a fear of heights and children should be supervised at all times due to the narrow towpath and wide gaps in the railings.
START Trevor Basin [SJ 272423].
DIRECTIONS See Walk 6.

The Pontcysyllte aqueduct, built between 1795 – 1805 by Thomas Telford in conjunction with William Jessop, is both a masterpiece of engineering and a structure of beauty. Its grand opening attracted thousands of people. It carries the canal 126 feet above the river Dee in a cast iron trough 1007 feet long, 11 feet 10 inches wide, 5 feet 3 inches deep and ¾ inches thick, held in place by the weight of water and supported by 18 slender tapering partly hollow stone piers. The mortar used was made of oxen blood, lime and water. Welsh Flannel dipped in boiling sugar and lead sealed the joints. The iron castings were made at nearby Cefn Mawr. It was the highest navigable aqueduct in the world and was built to extend the canal to the Dee at Chester, but this never happened due mainly to difficult terrain and rising costs. For information on Trevor Basin see Walk 7.

Follow the canal across the stunning aqueduct high above the Dee valley. Continue along the towpath, then cross a footbridge adjoining a lift bridge over the canal. Turn RIGHT along the canalside lane to a small car park. (For Walk B continue beside the canal then pass under the end of the aqueduct and return across it to Trevor Basin.) For Walk

A join the nearby B5434 and follow it down to cross the ancient stone bridge over the Dee. Follow the road RIGHT, then take the Offa's Dyke Path on the left past the end of Glandwr up to the canal. Follow it RIGHT, then cross footbridge 32W and continue to the nearby road. Turn LEFT then go through a gate opposite and through the Anglo Welsh car park to cross a footbridge over the canal in Trevor Basin.

WALK 12

TY MAWR COUNTRY PARK

DESCRIPTION A 5¼ mile (A) or 4½ mile (B) walk featuring the canal, the beautiful river Dee, a Country Park and two major engineering structures. The route follows the canal across the famous Pontcysyllte aqueduct, then eastwards to the B5605. Here Walk B short cuts the main route which continues south along the canal, before heading back to join the B5605. After passing through Newbridge it continues to Ty Mawr Country Park. From the impressive 19thC Cefn railway viaduct it follows the river Dee to the aqueduct and climbs beneath it to Trevor Basin. Allow about 3 hours.
START Trevor Basin [SJ 272423] or Ty Mawr Country Park [SJ 283414].
DIRECTIONS For Trevor Basin see Walk 6. Ty Mawr is reached from the B5605 near Cefn Mawr.

12

1 From Trevor Basin follow the canal across Pontcysyllte Aqueduct over the river Dee. Shortly it bends past a liftbridge/ footbridge at Froncysyllte and continues eastwards, later bending towards bridge 27W. (For Walk B go up to the nearby B5605 and turn left along the pavement, over the railway, and on past Pentre to point 3.)

2 Follow the canal under the bridge, and shortly under bridge 26W. Just before Whitehouse Tunnel take a path angling left up through trees, past the tunnel entrance and on to the A5. Turn LEFT along the protected pavement, then LEFT again along the road through Bryn-yr-Eos. Just before it bends left go through a kissing gate on the right and a nearby field gate, then go up the middle of the field to another kissing gate. Follow the boundary on your left to a stile/ gates, then go along the next field edge to a kissing gate and an enclosed path to a road junction in Pentre. Follow the road ahead through the village to the B5605. Cross the road and turn RIGHT.

3 Continue along the pavement, over the river Dee and up through Newbridge. Turn LEFT along Cae Gwilym Lane through the railway arch and on to Ty Mawr Country Park. *Nearby Cefn Mawr once had an ironworks and a colliery.* Go through the entrance and to the Visitor Centre ahead.

4 From the Visitor Centre go past a large outbuilding, bending left past its end to a gate (2E). Follow the path down past small animal enclosures to a gate (3L) and down through Mini Beast Wood to a gate at a track and one opposite by a nearby dovecote. Follow the surfaced path towards Cefn viaduct, soon beneath its towering arches. *Standing 147 feet high, with 19 arches, the viaduct, which carries the Chester-Shrewsbury railway line, was built in 1848 by Henry Robertson. One of the first trains across, full of VIPs, apparently broke down and was stranded in the middle overnight!* The path now heads west near the tree-lined river Dee. Later, just before the path bends up right, go down a stepped path on the left. Follow the waymarked path near the river through fields to eventually reach a track at a finger post. Turn LEFT over a stream and continue past the riverbank – *offering a good view of the aqueduct* – to a finger post. (Here you can follow an alternative route (b) signposted 'Aqueduct Viewpoint Walk' to Trevor Basin.) The main route (a) continues ahead on the wooded riverside path, then follows a stepped path up beneath the aqueduct, at a path junction bearing RIGHT up to the canal.

13

CHIRK CASTLE

DESCRIPTION A 7 mile walk from the small border town of Chirk, featuring a fascinating World Heritage section of canal, the Offa's Dyke Path (ODP), and a 14thC castle. The route joins the canal at Chirk Bank, then follows it across Chirk Aqueduct, through the long Chirk Tunnel, known as 'The Darkie' (a railed towpath but bring a torch, or use an alternative road route) past a marina and through a shorter tunnel. After a section of the ODP it follows a permissive National Trust path (open 1st April – 30th September) across Chirk Castle estate, with the option of visiting the Castle & gardens (check opening times), before returning to Chirk. Allow about 3 ½ hours.

START Chirk car park [SJ291377].

DIRECTIONS From the B5070 in Chirk go along Colliery Road, signposted Pont-y-Blew/car park, then first right (Pwll y waun) to find the large car park and toilets near Castle Health Centre and behind The Hand Hotel.

*C*hirk *stands in Wales overlooking the border with England. Its strategic importance is evidenced by a 12thC Norman castle and the more famous Chirk castle to the west completed in 1310 by Roger Mortimer for Edward I after the conquest of Wales. It was one of a chain of border castles built to reinforce English dominance. Now managed by the National Trust, it has been continuously occupied by the Myddleton family since 1595. Chirk is also situated on Thomas Telford's historic London to Holyhead turnpike road, along which stagecoaches carried the Irish Mail. Coal mining has been important to the town and surrounding area since the 16thC, with the last local colliery closing in 1968.*

I Leave the car park at the far 'no exit' corner to pass through the Hand Hotel's car park, then turn LEFT along the main road. Go past shops to St Mary's Church – *parts of which date from the 12thC. Behind The Mount, the prominent 18thC three storey house on the corner, is the site of the*

Norman motte and bailey castle which protected the ford over the river Ceiriog. In 1164 it resisted Henry II, whose army was subsequently defeated by the Welsh at Crogen 2 miles to the west of Chirk. Continue down the pavement beside the B5070 to cross a stile on the left. Follow the path down the field to a stile and on through trees to rejoin the B5070 at the entrance to Divine Dreams, *a former mill.*

2 Turn LEFT along the pavement opposite, over the river Ceiriog into Shropshire. Go past The Bridge Inn and up the side road (Weston Rhyn) into Chirk Bank. Just before the road bridge turn RIGHT along an access lane beside the canal to houses, then continue across Chirk Aqueduct into Wales (For information see Walk 14). The main route follows the railed towpath through the Chirk Tunnel. (An alternative is to go up to the B4500 then continue along nearby Station Road. At the roundabout by the station turn left over the railway then descend a path on the right down to the canal near the tunnel entrance.) *The 1377 feet/420 metre long straight tunnel, the longest of on the canal, was completed in 1801, with the central section excavated from two shafts. Chirk and Whitehouse tunnels were reputedly the first in Britain to have towpaths, making passage through quicker.* Continue along the delightful mature wooded section of the canal, then a more open section past Chirk Marina, through Whitehouse Tunnel (574 feet/175 metres) and under bridge 26W.

3 After bridge 27W, where the canal bends west, turn sharp RIGHT up the way-marked Offa's Dyke Path to the B5605. Turn RIGHT over the canal, through a kissing gate and a gateway ahead. The ODP crosses a field to a gate, then the mid-slopes of the next field to a kissing gate. It angles LEFT through the tree boundary to another kissing gate and goes up the field edge, soon alongside the earthwork of Offa's Dyke, to a kissing gate. Go down the track to a gate and past Cloud Hill's entrance to the A5. Turn RIGHT briefly along the pavement, then cross the road with care to a stone stile opposite and gate below. Follow the gated

ODP through fields and on to a narrow road. Follow it LEFT, through crossroads, then up to join another road. Soon, at a farm the signposted ODP turns RIGHT briefly along a track to a kissing gate then continues across two fields to a road. Follow it RIGHT – *soon with a view of Chirk Castle.* On the bend by Rose Cottage turn LEFT and follow the National Trust permissive path past Tyn-y-Groes, then along the edge of three fields and past the large car park to the Visitor Centre.

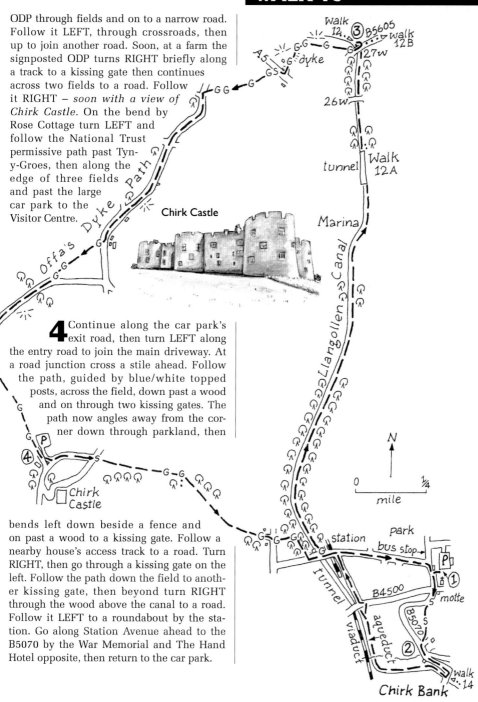

Chirk Castle

4 Continue along the car park's exit road, then turn LEFT along the entry road to join the main driveway. At a road junction cross a stile ahead. Follow the path, guided by blue/white topped posts, across the field, down past a wood and on through two kissing gates. The path now angles away from the corner down through parkland, then

bends left down beside a fence and on past a wood to a kissing gate. Follow a nearby house's access track to a road. Turn RIGHT, then go through a kissing gate on the left. Follow the path down the field to another kissing gate, then beyond turn RIGHT through the wood above the canal to a road. Follow it LEFT to a roundabout by the station. Go along Station Avenue ahead to the B5070 by the War Memorial and The Hand Hotel opposite, then return to the car park.

WALK 14

CHIRK AQUEDUCT

DESCRIPTION A meandering 4½ mile **(A)** or 3 mile **(B)** walk featuring two engineering structures of different transport eras crossing the border between England and Wales. The route goes along the part wooded Ceiriog valley, passing under Thomas Telford's less well known, but equally splendid Chirk Aqueduct and adjoining railway viaduct. From Pont Faen it follows a section of the Shropshire Way to Chirk Bank, where Walk B leaves, and on to Rhoswiel, It then returns along the canal past The Poacher's pub to Chirk Bank and on over Chirk Aqueduct into Chirk. Allow about 2½ hours.
START Chirk car park [SJ291377].
DESCRIPTION See Walk 13.

The attractive 710 feet long ten-arched Chirk Aqueduct carries the canal in a cast iron trough 70 feet above the Ceiriog valley. Begun in 1796 it was completed in 1801, providing a transport link for local coalmines and quarries. Adjoining it is the railway viaduct built by Henry Robertson in 1846-48 for the Chester-Shrewsbury railway line. It was made deliberately higher than the aqueduct to emphasise the superiority of rail over water! Due to the objection of Col. Robert Myddleton Biddulph of Chirk Castle it was built at night! Both are built of local yellow sandstone.

I Follow instructions in paragraph 1 of Walk 13.

2 Go through a kissing gate opposite, then across the field near the Ceiriog river to pass under the massive stone Chirk Aqueduct and railway viaduct. Continue along the river bank to eventually reach a road junction. Turn LEFT across Pont Faen – *the oldest stone bridge in the Ceiriog valley and once an important crossing on the Chester to Cardiff road* – and past the side road to the hamlet of Pont Faen. Continue up the road, then turn LEFT along a side road past Yew Tree cottages and on beneath woodland. Take

the signposted Shropshire Way angling left through mature woodland and across a steep wooded slope to a stile. Follow the stiled path between fences, along a field edge, then across the railway line. The path continues along the edge of a large field – *with Llangollen Canal visible below* – then bends right across to a small gate onto a track. Go through another small gate opposite and along a hedged path down to a road at the small community of Chirk Bank. (For Walk B turn left down the road to join the canal.)

3 Turn RIGHT up the road, then LEFT briefly along Oaklands Road to go through a gate on the right into a large field. Go past the tree boundary corner ahead, then a way-marked post to a kissing gate ahead. Go across the next field to a stile in the hedge ahead just beyond its corner. Follow the embanked path through trees to another stile ahead. Go up the large field to a stile then across the next field to a stile near its left-hand corner. Go past the side and end of the building, then along a rough lane past houses to the road in Rhoswiel. Turn LEFT to cross the bridge over the canal, then descend to the towpath. Follow the canal northwards past The Poacher's pub to road bridge 21 in Chirk Bank. Now follow an access lane beside the canal to houses, then continue along the towpath and across Chirk Aqueduct into Wales. At the entrance to Chirk Tunnel take the wide pathway up to Castle Road. Follow it right past a café to the B5070 opposite St Mary's church.

WALK 15

CHIRK BANK TO TREVOR BASIN

DESCRIPTION A 5¼ mile linear walk, combined with bus 64, featuring the main engineering highlights of the World Heritage Site – the Pontcysyllte (at beginning and end) and Chirk Aqueducts, two tunnels (bring a torch). Allow about 3 hours.
START Trevor Basin [SJ 272423]. See Walk 6.

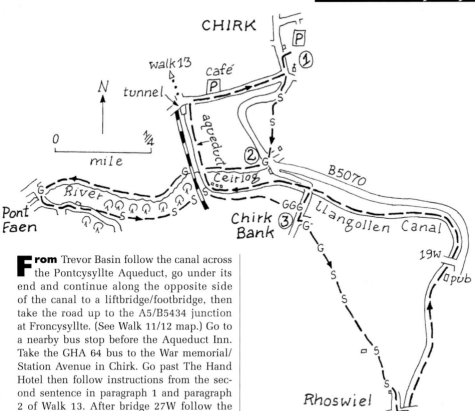

rom Trevor Basin follow the canal across the Pontcysyllte Aqueduct, go under its end and continue along the opposite side of the canal to a liftbridge/footbridge, then take the road up to the A5/B5434 junction at Froncysyllte. (See Walk 11/12 map.) Go to a nearby bus stop before the Aqueduct Inn. Take the GHA 64 bus to the War memorial/Station Avenue in Chirk. Go past The Hand Hotel then follow instructions from the second sentence in paragraph 1 and paragraph 2 of Walk 13. After bridge 27W follow the canal west to Froncysyllte and back across the Pontcysyllte Aqueduct.

WALK 16

LLANGOLLEN TO CHIRK BANK

DESCRIPTION An 11 mile linear walk along most of the World Heritage Site canal, featuring the Pontcysllte and Chirk Aqueducts and two tunnels (*bring a torch*). Park in Chirk car park (See Walk 13) then catch the GHA 64 bus from near the War Memorial junction with Station Avenue (See Walk 13 map) to Parade Street, Llangollen. Allow about 5½ hours. This walk can easily be done in reverse.

START Llangollen Bridge [SJ215422].

eferring to Walk 9 map cross the bridge over the river and turn LEFT along the pavement opposite, then RIGHT on a signposted path, taking its right fork up to Llangollen Wharf. Now follow the canal eastwards to Trevor Basin then across Pontcysllte Aqueduct to Froncysyllte. Referring to Walk 12 map continue along the canal to bridge 27W. Now referring to Walk 13 map follow the canal south through Whitehouse Tunnel and the longer Chirk Tunnel (road alternative), then across Chirk Aqueduct to Chirk Bank. Turn left down the road to the B5470. Follow the pavement over the river Ceiriog then cross to the entrance to Divine Dreams opposite. Follow a path left to a stile and up a field to rejoin the B5470 into Chirk.

17

IFTON MEADOWS

DESCRIPTION A varied 4¼ mile way-marked Shropshire Way Circular Walk (SWCW) around St Martin's in north Shropshire. The route passes through Ifton Meadows, a Local Nature Reserve offering good views, then descends into a narrow wooded valley. After a short steep climb it continues south, soon on the Wat's Dyke Way, then returns along the canal and across farmland. Allow about 2½ hours. Café in Superstore.

START Car park opposite Stan's Superstore, St Martin's [SJ 324368].

DIRECTIONS The large supermarket adjoins the B5069 near the junction with the B5068. Parking is allowed.

St Martin's developed into an important coalmining community around Ifton Colliery, first sunk in 1771, which became the largest in Shropshire, at its peak employing over 1300 men. In 1968 the colliery closed, the pit became an industrial estate and the reclaimed spoil heap a Local Nature Reserve. Near the start is the old Ifton Miners Welfare Institute, affectionately known as The Stute.

I From the car park entrance turn RIGHT along the pavement past the garage and through a kissing gate. Turn LEFT and follow the kissing gated path along the edge of two fields and across another to a narrow hedge/tree lined lane. Follow it RIGHT to staggered crossroads by Pentre Nurseries. Go along the road signposted to Pentre/ Ifton Meadows Local Nature Reserve. At the entrance to Old Ifton industrial estate – *on the site of the former colliery* – turn LEFT to a small car park and kissing gate into the Reserve. Follow the waymarked wide surfaced path past an information board through the former colliery site, soon rising and becoming a narrower stony path. Shortly it bends north – *with good views* – up to a circular coloured ceramic tile design on the ground.

2 Go to a small waymark post ahead and turn LEFT past the right side of a tree. Ignore a clear path to your left and continue straight ahead on a fainter path down towards the wooded valley, soon joined by a path on the left, to reach a nearby way-marked path junction. Take its left fork ahead, soon angling half-right to a cross-path at another post. Follow it LEFT to a kissing gate/gate. Just ahead turn RIGHT down a nearby house's stony access track through trees to a narrow road. Turn LEFT up to a junction, then follow the signposted SWCW along the road ahead to cross a small 18thC stone bridge over Morlas Brook. Continue up the road to a junction by Keeper's Cottage. Follow the road south through mature woodland, past a farm and other dwellings, then cross a stile on the left to join a section of Wat's Dyke Way. Follow the waymarked path along the field edge and across the field passing to the right of a telegraph pole to a stile. Turn LEFT along the narrow tree-lined green track, soon descending steadily and bending right. *In the wood to your left are the remains of Wat's Dyke. Near it is the former World War II Bank Top prisoner of war camp, which housed 600 men.* The track then becomes a lane and passes cottages to reach the B5070.

3 Cross the road and turn LEFT across the bridge, then RIGHT on the signposted SWCW/Wat's Dyke Way along a stony access track past a house above former Escob Mill and up to a stile/gate at the last outbuilding. Go across the field to a stile into woodland. Follow the stepped path up onto the former Ellesmere-Oswestry railway embankment and down to a stile. Angle RIGHT to a stile/bridge/stile at the nearby wood corner. The path continues along the field edge to a stile just before the corner, then rises left through trees to reach bridge 15W over the canal. Go under the bridge and follow the tree-lined canal eastwards, passing under bridges 14W and 13W and past a cottage and a house opposite.

4 Just before the canal begins to bend half-right, turn LEFT to cross a large gated footbridge. Go along the field edge to a kissing gate onto a green track and to a kissing gate ahead. Follow the path up through the field to a waymarked boundary corner, then beside the tree boundary to a kissing gate. Go along the right-hand edge of the next field and on to a kissing gate ahead. Go along the narrow enclosed path between houses, then an access road. At the junction turn RIGHT along the road past 13thC St Martin's Parish Church then LEFT along Green Lane. Just before the junction with Overton Road follow a path angling left through the Memorial Garden to a zebra crossing and the nearby car park.

WALK 18

CHIRK TO ELLESMERE

DESCRIPTION An 11 mile linear walk along the canal from Chirk to Ellesmere, featuring a crossing of Chirk Aqueduct and several canalside pubs. Park in Ellesmere town centre car park and take the 53 or 449 bus to Oswestry, then the 2/2A to Chirk. Allow about 5 hours.
START St Mary's Church, Chirk [SJ 291376].

Initially referring to Walk 14 map, from the church go along the B4500 (Castle Road) opposite then take a path down to the canal by the entrance to Chirk Tunnel. Follow the canal across the nearby Chirk Aqueduct to Chirk Bank. Continue with the canal past The Poacher's pub (bridge 19), the Lion Quay's Hotel (bridge 17), the Jack Mytton Inn (bridge 11) and the Narrowboat Inn (bridge 5) to the junction with the Montgomery Canal at

An old coal truck

Lower Frankton. Referring to Walks 19 and 21 maps continue along the Llangollen Canal to another junction at Ellesmere. Bear left along the short canal branch. Head along Wharf Road into the town centre.

FRANKTON JUNCTION

DESCRIPTION A 3¾ mile (**A**) or 2½ mile (**B**) walk from the junction of the Llangollen and Montgomery Canals. The route follows the waymarked Shropshire Way across fields, then returns along the Llangollen Canal. Walk A then extends along the narrower Montgomery Canal past Frankton Locks to its disused Weston Branch, before returning. Allow about 2 hours. Frankton Locks operate between 12.00-14.00 daily, so I recommend that you coincide your walk with this busy boating period.

START Car park, Lower Frankton [SJ 371318].

DIRECTIONS At Welsh Frankton on the A495 take a minor road signposted to Lower Frankton. At a second junction just beyond Holly House turn left along the no through road to cross a bridge over the canal by Bridge Cottage. Turn right into a small car park.

The Montgomery Canal section from Frankton Junction to just south of Llanymynech was built as a branch of the Ellesmere Canal in the mid 1790s primarily to carry limestone quarried at Llanymynech to canalside kilns to produce lime for fertilizer to enrich farmland. The canal connected with the new Montgomeryshire Canal which extended south to Welshpool, finally reaching Newtown in 1819. Later, trade gradually declined due to competition from the railways. It fell into disuse after it breached in 1936 and was closed in 1944. Since 1969 sections of the canal have gradually been restored.

I Go back across the bridge and along the road, soon bending left, then turn RIGHT on the signposted Shropshire Way along an access road. Follow it up to its end at Oakwood to gates ahead into a field. Go half-RIGHT and follow the waymarked stiled path through several fields, then, at the boundary of a house, left round the field edge. Cross two forks of the house's driveway and follow the narrow waymarked path ahead between boundaries to a kissing gate to join the canal by bridge 63.

2 Turn RIGHT and follow the canal back to Lower Frankton. Go under bridge 69. (For Walk B a small gate gives access to the road.) Continue along the towpath past the junction to a gate. Cross road bridge 1W then turn LEFT through a gate and follow the towpath along the Montgomery Canal past Frankton Locks to the old Weston Branch just before bridge 71. Return to cross a small bridge over the top narrow lock. Go past the utility building and along the stony track to the car park.

WELSH FRANKTON TO ELLESMERE

DESCRIPTION A 5 mile linear walk along the tranquil canal from the Narrowboat Inn, Welsh Frankton to Ellesmere. Refer to Walks 19/21 maps. Allow about 2½ hours.

START Narrowboat Inn, Welsh Frankton [SJ 353325].

Take the hourly 449 bus from Cross street, Ellesmere to the Narrowboat Inn on the A495. Follow the Llangollen Canal past its junction with the Montgomery Canal at Lower Frankton to another junction. Bear left along the short branch Ellesmere Branch Canal. At its end bear right along nearby Wharf Road into the town centre.

WALK 21

ELLESMERE

DESCRIPTION A varied 2½ mile walk around Ellesmere, featuring a delightful woodland walk by The Mere, a lakeside café, a small woodland nature reserve, and canal sections. Allow about 1½ hours.

START The Square, Ellesmere [SJ 400348]

DIRECTIONS The area known as The Square is by the old Town Hall at the intersection of Cross, High, Scotland and Market Streets. Cross Street car park is nearby.

*E*llesmere is a small attractive mar- ket town of Saxon origin, lying near The Mere, the largest of nine glacial meres in the area. Roger de Montgomery, Earl of Shrewsbury built a motte and bailey castle here after 1086. Afterwards its ownership changed many times and it was abandoned in the 14thC. The town developed around the castle and St Mary's church and was granted a charter by Henry III in 1221 to hold weekly markets. The town's prosperity was enhanced later for a while by the opening of the Ellesmere Canal, then a railway in the 1860s connecting it with Oswestry and Whitchurch. Nowadays, its interesting buildings and beautiful lake attract many visitors each year (See Walk 24).

I Go along High Street, then at cross- roads turn LEFT along one way Watergate Street. At the junction turn RIGHT then cross the road by the Pelican Crossing. Turn RIGHT, then LEFT along a signposted path to a finger post by a stony cross-path in Cremorne Gardens, with The Mere just ahead. Turn LEFT and follow the wide path along the wooded eastern side of the large lake to a kissing gate just beyond its corner. Return to the finger post and continue ahead to leave Cremorne Gardens, then follow a lakeside promenade to The Boathouse. Join the nearby pavement and cross the road by

a Pelican Crossing to a kissing gate oppo- site. Follow the wide path leading left up to a kissing gate. Just beyond take the way- marked Shropshire Way grass path up the slope and on near a fence to kissing gates at a lane into The Plantation Nature Reserve. Go up a stepped path to a path junction. Take the waymarked SW right fork down through trees, soon bending left and continu- ing down and along the edge of the wood to an information board, then beside a fence to the canal. Turn RIGHT.

2 Follow the canal past the marina to its junction with the Ellesmere Branch sec-

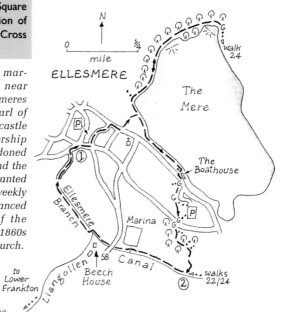

tion. The large red-bricked Beech House opposite was built in 1805 as the Ellesmere Canal Company head office. It contained a corner committee room on the ground floor, designed to overlook the three arms of the canal. It is believed that Thomas Telford stayed here. Adjoining the house was a main- tenance yard, containing a dry dock and workshops. It is still used today by the Canal and River Trust. Cross footbridge 59 over the Ellesmere Branch and follow it to its end. Bear RIGHT to follow nearby Wharf Road to a T- junction. Turn RIGHT to the start.

THREE MERES

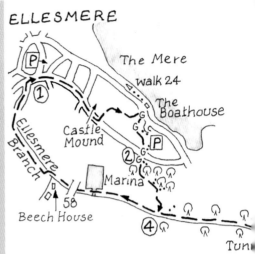

ELLESMERE

The Mere
walk 24
The Boathouse
Castle Mound
Marina
58
Beech House
Tun

DESCRIPTION A 6¾ mile (**A**) or 6 mile (**B**) walk along one of the most attractive wooded sections of the Llangollen Canal through part of Shropshire's 'Lake District'. The route, a section of the Shropshire Way (SW), heads to Castlefields Meadow overlooking The Mere, then passes through a small woodland nature reserve to join the canal. It follows it past Blake Mere, then completes a circuit of beautiful Cole Mere (Walk B leaves it earlier), now a Country Park. It returns along the canal, continuing past the marina and along the short Ellesmere Branch. Allow about 3½ hours. For information on Ellesmere see Walk 21.

START The Square, Ellesmere [SJ 400348] or Castlefields car park [SJ 406344].

DIRECTIONS See Walk 21. For Castlefields car park see Walk 23. From its south west corner take a path up to kissing gates at a lane into The Plantation at point 2.

1 Go along High Street. At crossroads go up St John's Hill ahead, past side roads. At a junction with Love Lane go up the road ahead. At Rosebank turn LEFT up the stepped path to a kissing gate into Castlefields Meadow – *the site of the motte and bailey castle.* Follow the path ahead – *soon with a view of The Mere* – down to a chained rock sculpture. Bend RIGHT with the path, soon taking the left fork past another sculpture down towards the lake. At a crossroad of paths turn LEFT to a kissing gate by the road. *Nearby is The Boathouse café and Visitor Centre, with its delightful lakeside garden.* Turn RIGHT along a surfaced path up to a kissing gate. Just beyond take the waymarked SW grass path angling RIGHT up the slope (or if starting from Castlefields car park follow the path ahead to it) and on near a fence to kissing gates at a lane into the Plantation Nature Reserve.

2 Go up the stepped path then take the waymarked SW right fork down through trees, soon bending left and continuing down and along the edge of the wood to an infor-

mation board, then beside a fence to the canal. Turn LEFT along the towpath, shortly passing through Ellesmere Tunnel – *87 yards/80 metres long with a railed towpath. You might be accompanied by a boat passing through with its headlight on.* Follow the canal past Blake Mere, under bridges 56 and 55 and past Cole Mere – *with glimpses of the lake through adjoining Yell Wood. Lime and coal was off-loaded here for lime-kilns in the wood. The canal also carried cheese from local farms to the market in Ellesmere.*

3 After passing under bridge 54 take a stepped path up to cross the bridge to a Cole Mere welcome board. Either descend through the trees to join the wide trail path below and follow it LEFT through the mature woodland or follow a narrow path beside the canal, then down steps to join the main trail. The trail continues to small gates at the edge of the wood and a choice of paths. Follow the boardwalked path near the edge of the lake. *Cole Mere, mainly enclosed by mature woodland, with two flower rich hay meadows, provides a habitat for a variety of wildfowl, waders and other birds. It is the only place in England that supports the rare Least Water Lily. Yell Meadow is noted for its orchids. Across the lake is the 19thC Boat House, used for fishing and hunting groups, and now the Sailing Club. Both paths join to go through a kissing-gate at the end of the*

22

lake. Nearby is St John the Evangelist church, built in 1869, using Cefn stone transported along the canal from Trevor.

4 Turn RIGHT along the stony path, soon alongside the lake, to pass the Sailing Club. Continue with the path through Boat House Wood near the lake. When it splits you have a choice to rejoin the canal. (For Walk B keep ahead to a kissing gate, then go along a road past thatched timber-framed Little Mill Cottage and up across bridge 55 over the canal. Descend steps to the towpath.) For Walk A take the right fork to a

WALK 23

COLE MERE

DESCRIPTION A delightful 1¾ mile walk featuring three-quarters of the trail around Colemere Country Park and a short section of the Llangollen Canal. Allow about 1 hour.
START Colemere Country Park car park [SJ 436328].
DIRECTIONS The Country Park is signposted 1 mile from the A528, 2 miles south west of Ellesmere.

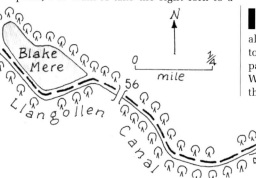

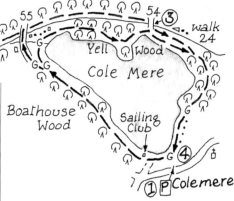

❙ Head to a kissing gate at the end of the lake (point 4 on the map). Turn LEFT along the stony path, soon alongside the lake, to pass the Sailing Club. Continue with the path through Boat House Wood near the lake. When it splits keep ahead to a kissing gate, then follow a road past Little Mill Cottage

nearby kissing gate and past the open end of the lake to another kissing gate and stream. At a stony track beyond turn RIGHT passing below a cottage. Take its right fork to continue with the wide stony path past an open aspect of the lake and on through woodland to join your outward route at the stump of a tree and cross bridge 54. Return along the canal towards Ellesmere to where you joined it.

5 Follow instructions in paragraph 2 of Walk 21.

and up across bridge 55 over the canal. Turn right down steps to the towpath and follow the canal to bridge 54. Now follow instructions in paragraph 3 of Walk 22.

Beech House

THE MERE

DESCRIPTION A 7 mile walk exploring the interesting countryside near the medieval market town Ellesmere, featuring glacial meres, woodland, an ancient village, and one of the most attractive sections of the Llangollen Canal. The route first passes along the side of The Mere then heads across undulating countryside to Welshampton, before returning on a section of the Shropshire Way along the part wooded/ tree-lined canal past Cole Mere and Blake Mere, then through a small woodland nature reserve. Allow about 4 hours. You can easily include a 1½ mile circuit around Cole Mere (See Walk 22).

START Castlefields car park, Ellesmere [SJ 406344].

DIRECTIONS The large signposted car park (all day fee) lies off the A525 just beyond the Pelican Crossing near The Boathouse by The Mere on the outskirts of Ellesmere. *Note that the gates close at 5.30 pm.*

The Mere is the largest of nine glacial meres in North Shropshire, formed at the end of the last Ice Age from melting ice. Lying on the edge of the medieval market town of Ellesmere, it is an important place for wildlife and a popular place for visitors, attracted by its beauty, Victorian Cremorne Gardens, woodland lakeside walk, rowing boats, steamboat trips and fishing. Moscow Island opposite The Boathouse Visitor Centre and café was formed in 1812 from extracted earth during road-building. It is home to up to 25 pairs of herons.

From the information board near the car park entrance follow a surfaced path above the road and down through two kissing gates to the main road by the Pelican Crossing. Go to the opposite side and turn LEFT past The Boathouse and its end to the edge of The Mere. Now follow the lakeside promenade northwards, then go through a gate into Cremorne Gardens and follow the wide path near The Mere. Continue on the signposted Woodland Walk near the northern edge of the lake, bending round its corner to a kissing gate. Follow a narrow lakeside path to another kissing gate, then through woodland to a fingerpost.

2 Turn LEFT and follow the narrow enclosed path, signposted to Welshampton, to a wide stony track. Follow it ahead to Crimps Farm. At a track junction just before the attractive three storey red-bricked house turn RIGHT on a signposted path along the stony track. When it bends left go to gates ahead into a field. Go up the slope – *at the top enjoying good views looking back* – then down to join a track to pass the end of a wood and a kissing gate. Leave the track and continue ahead by the fence to another kissing gate. Go across the field and down to a kissing gate. Go across the next field and up to a kissing gate/gate in its top left-hand corner. Descend a short green track, then at the tree boundary corner turn RIGHT along the field edge past a small pond and a waymarked fence corner by another nearby pond. Continue by the tree boundary to a kissing gate in it, then beside the boundary below a field edge. Turn RIGHT along an improving track to a former

24

farm. Pass between buildings to the A495 in Welshampton. Turn LEFT to a junction by the Primary School. Continue beside the main road past the Church of St Michael and All Angels oppo-

Continue along the canal passing under two more bridges then along the edge of Blake Mere. Afterwards the canal passes through Ellesmere Tunnel – *87 yards/80 metres long with a railed towpath. A modern sculpture refers you to the tunnel entrance where*

The Mere

site. *The church, built in 1863 on the site of earlier ones, was designed by the renowned Victorian architect Sir George Gilbert Scott, whose many icon buildings include the Terminus Hotel at St Pancras Station, the Albert Memorial and the Foreign Office in London.*

ropes from the horse-drawn boats cut into the stone. Continue along the towpath.

3 Just beyond turn RIGHT along Lyneal Lane. Follow it out of the village, then continue with the road to eventually reach a bridge (no. 51) over the canal. Descend to the towpath, go under the bridge and follow the canal under bridge 52 and past Llyneal Wharf. After bridge 53 it bends westwards, soon passing Yell Wood opposite and hidden Cole Mere. *Crossing Bridge 54 provides a sight of the lake and access to its circular trail (paragraphs 3 and 4 of Walk 22).*

4 At a stone sculpture turn RIGHT on a multi signed boardwalked path by a fence up to an information board on The Plantation, now a Nature Reserve, with an interesting WW II history. Continue with the path past a side path along the wood edge, soon rising and bending up through trees to a path junction. Descend LEFT to a kissing gate onto a lane. Go through the kissing gate opposite, then take the stepped path angling RIGHT down to the car park.

25

BETTISFIELD MOSS

DESCRIPTION A 4¼ mile walk along the canal towards Bettisfield, then returning on the waymarked Shropshire Way through Bettisfield Moss, part of a National Nature Reserve, and a section of the Prees Branch Canal. Allow about 2¼ hours.

START Car park by Morris' lift bridge 45 [SJ 493354].

DIRECTIONS See Walk 27.

Fenn's, Whixall and Bettisfield Mosses National Nature Reserve, an SSSI, straddles the border of England and Wales. It is the third largest lowland raised peat bog in Britain, formed at the end of the last Ice Age. For centuries peat was cut in the Mosses primarily as fuel for domestic use, but it was the arrival of the canal – carried across on a floating bed – then the railways, providing an accessible means of transporting the peat to markets, that greatly increased the scale of activity. Rescued in 1990 from destruction by large-scale commercial mechanical peat-cutting and drainage, it has been intensively restored and is now an internationally recognised habitat for bog plants and wildlife, some rare. Among those now thriving are butterflies, moths, dragonflies, adders, common lizards, and wetland birds.

1 From the lift bridge head west along the towpath, shortly passing under Bridge 46 at the junction with the Prees Branch Canal. *This was a roving bridge that allowed horses towing laden canal boats to cross the canal without needing to be unhitched.* Continue along a straight section of the main canal, shortly lined by woodland. At the end of the surfaced towpath follow a short boardwalked path to a viewing platform with seats and an information board on the Mosses National Nature Reserve. *Here you can appreciate the expansive area of restored mosses.* Return to continue along the canal – *soon passing a view opposite into Bettisfield Moss, then a post indicating you are crossing the border into Wales.* Later the canal becomes more open.

Bettisfield

2 Cross Bridge 47 and follow the waymarked Shropshire Way (SW) path across three fields to a road. Follow it LEFT. At a junction turn LEFT along a rougher road, soon bending right, then continue along the right of two stony tracks past Moss Poldings to its end by other houses. Continue ahead along a wide tree-lined path past a small wood then turn LEFT to a kissing gate into Bettisfield Moss. Follow the path past an information board and along the edge of the Reserve. Shortly, the waymarked SW bends right and follows a faint green track through woodland. When it bends right the waymarked SW continues ahead along the woodland edge to another information board at the Reserve corner. Follow a path ahead through bracken and trees to a stony access track.

3 Follow it ahead to Brookhouse. Turn LEFT with the SW along a track past a barn, then angle across a field to a gate in its right-hand corner by a house. Cross nearby lift bridge no. 1 over the Prees Branch Canal. Turn LEFT along the towpath to the junction with the main canal. Cross bridge 46 to rejoin your outward route.

PREES BRANCH CANAL

DESCRIPTION A 5 mile walk featuring the delightful attractive narrow branch canal, with its unrestored section a hidden gem of a Nature Reserve, run by Shropshire Wildlife Trust. The route follows short sections of both canals, then explores the adjoining countryside before rejoining the Prees Branch to reach Whixall Marina. It continues for over ½ mile further along the old canal, stunning in summer with its rich plant life, then returns along quiet country

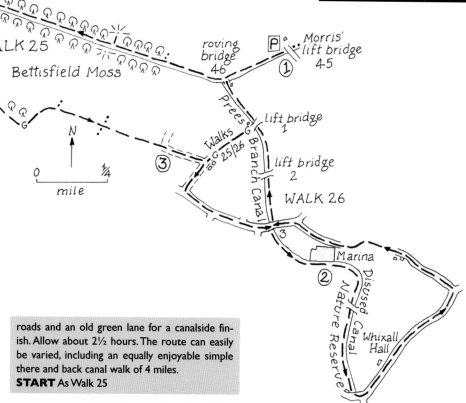

roads and an old green lane for a canalside finish. Allow about 2½ hours. The route can easily be varied, including an equally enjoyable simple there and back canal walk of 4 miles.
START As Walk 25

*T**he Prees Branch** was only built as far as Quina Brook due to a lack of finance. It is now only navigable for almost a mile to Whixall marina, built a few decades ago from a clay pit that provided puddle clay to line local canals. The next short section of the old canal is now an important nature reserve, with rich flora.*

From the Lift Bridge follow the canal westwards, then cross bridge 46 – a roving bridge that allowed horses towing laden canal boats to cross the canal without needing to be unhitched – and go along the towpath of the adjoining Prees Branch Canal. Shortly cross lift bridge 1 and follow the waymarked Shropshire Way through a nearby gate by a house and half-RIGHT across the large field to a gate. Follow a track past a barn to a track junction at Brookhouse. Follow its access track ahead to a road. Turn LEFT, then at the junction go along the road ahead past side roads to Dobson's Bridge no. 3 over the Prees Branch Canal. Turn RIGHT along the towpath to the large Whixall Marina.

2 Continue beside the old canal, still containing water but now edged by wild flowers, especially the yellow iris, passing under bridge 4 and eventually reaching a road. Turn LEFT past the side road and Whixall Hall. At the next junction turn LEFT along the road to its end at Alders Farm. Continue ahead along the track past outbuildings, then when it bends left keep ahead along a rough hedge-lined green track (Alders Lane) later improving as it rises to join a road. Go up the road past the Marina entrance to a junction. Turn LEFT to reach Dobson's Bridge. Descend steps on the left and go under the bridge then follow the canal north past lift bridge 2 to join your outward route at lift bridge 1.

WALK 27
WHIXALL & FENN'S MOSSES 1

DESCRIPTION A 3¼ mile (**A**) or 1¼ mile (**B**) walk following waymarked green and purple trails around Whixall Moss – part of Fenn's, Whixall and Bettisfield Mosses National Nature Reserve (See Walk 25) – then returning along the canal. Allow about 2 hours. Detailed trail leaflets in dispensers available at start. Also online from 'publications.naturalengland.org.uk'.
START Car park by Morris' Lift Bridge 45 [SJ 493354].
DIRECTIONS The Nature Reserve is sign-posted from the Ellesmere – Whitchurch (A525), Wem – Whitchurch (B5476) and Wem –Welshampton (B5063) roads.

1 Follow the track past the nearby bunga-low to an information board on Allmark's Peat Mill (A), then on to a facing gate into the Reserve. Continue through woodland to a crossroad of tracks by Mosses Trail post 8. Turn LEFT with the green trail across Whixall Moss to a track T-junction by a pool at post 9. (For Walk B turn left and follow the meandering green trail to the canal. Follow it left past the Prees Branch Canal to the start.)

2 Turn RIGHT and follow the purple trail across the expansive area of moss. At a cross-road of tracks, by an owl sculpture at post 18 you cross the border into Wales. Follow the green track ahead past an infor-mation board on 'The Military of the Mosses' and side tracks. At post 16 turn LEFT across a sleeper bridge and continue by a line of trees and drainage ditch, then later through open woodland After post 15, the trail con-tinues with a path through trees to unexpect-edly reach the canal.

3 Turn LEFT along the straight wooded sec-tion of the canal, shortly having a brief view into Bettisfield Moss and crossing the border back into England. Soon afterwards you reach the stone surfaced towpath. Here take a short diversion along a boardwalked

path to a viewing platform with seats and an information board – *a good place for a break.* Afterwards resume your journey along the canal, shortly being joined by Walk B at the wood corner. Follow the canal past the Prees Branch Canal, under Whixall Moss Bridge 46 – *a roving bridge that allowed horses towing laden canal boats to cross the canal without needing to be unhitched* – and back to the start.

WALK 28
WHIXALL & FENN'S MOSSES 2

DESCRIPTION A fascinating meandering 4½ mile walk (**A**) combining the Orange Mosses's Trail (MT)/Shropshire Way (SW) and History Trail (HT) around part of Fenn's, Whixall and Bettisfield Mosses National Nature Reserve (See Walk 25), featuring a secret World War II Starfish Site (burning decoys to confuse German bombers), then returning along the canal. Allow about 2½ hours. Until 1990 the Mosses echoed to the sound of extensive commercial peat-cutting, and during both World Wars of gun-fire from military training exercises, but this restored unique wetland wilderness is now peaceful, supporting a wide variety of species. Included is a shorter 3½ mile walk (**B**) and the 1¾ mile Orange Trail (**C**) walk. Detailed trail leaflets in dispensers available at start. Also online from 'publications.naturalengland.org.uk'.
START Roundthorne Bridge, Whixall Moss [SJ 501357].
DIRECTIONS See Walk 29.

1 Head eastwards along the stony canalside track then go through gates on the left, waymarked SW/MT, to an information board on Whixall Marl Allotment. Continue along the trail round to a small gate. Turn RIGHT with the SW along a green track to a gate into the National Nature Reserve. Follow the wide green path to another gate, past a side path beyond, then woodland into a more open area of the vast Reserve.

2 At MT post 6 turn LEFT on the way-marked SW along a narrow green track, past a bench seat, now on the History Trail. At MT post 7, turn RIGHT to HT post 2. (For Walk C continue westwards with the MT/SW as described from the middle of paragraph 4.) Follow the trail past a pool to HT post 4. *Near here during the 19thC the well preserved bodies of a man and woman from the Iron Age, and a man from the Bronze Age were found. The*

trail meanders across Whixall Moss, at post 10 passing over the border into Wales and Fenn's Moss. It continues past a large area of restored commercial peatcutting and a nearby weather station – *used for climate change monitoring of peat, which contains great amounts of carbon* – to post 12. Turn LEFT along a former narrow gauge railway to nearby post 13. *The small concrete slab, one of many, supported fire baskets in 1940 prior to the creation of the more complex Starfish Site.* Return to post 12 and continue to post 14 by the nearby Starfish Site with an information board on this secret innovative World War II military site. Continue along a long section of the trail to post 15.

3 Turn RIGHT along the line of a pre-World War 1 horse-drawn tramway used for moving peat to a small factory sited by post 18, past post 16, an information board on the history of the military on the Mosses and post 17. Shortly follow a narrow stony track through open woodland to an information board. Just beyond nearby post 18 turn LEFT along a path through trees to post 19. Turn LEFT along the green cross-track – *another old tramway* – to post 20 – *the site of a*

lookout tower for the WWII bombing range. Return along the green track to the bend of the stony one left earlier at post 21. Follow it ahead to a gate and past Fenn's Cottage – *the office for the first peat factory.* Go along its access road past cottages – *built for peat workers in 1897* – to a junction. Turn RIGHT past more cottages then follow a stony track ahead to a junction. (For Walk B follow the track leading left to the canal and the start.)

4 Follow the signposted trails along the stony track ahead to a farm then along a green track, through a gate and on to an information board at post 1 by the former WWII battery shed. Go through a gate ahead and follow the green track through the Reserve. At a post turn LEFT with the MT along the narrow green track to join your outward route at point 2. Turn RIGHT along the MT/SW previously walked, then continue with the waymarked SW westwards on a wide trackway across the open moss. At MT post 8 turn LEFT on the SW between woodland to a gate to leave the Reserve. Follow the green track ahead past an information board on Allmark's Peat Mill to the small car park and canal at Morris Lift Bridge 45. Follow the canal back to the start.

HOLLINWOOD

DESCRIPTION A 7 mile walk exploring an attractive area of North Shropshire. Starting from the canal the route follows the new Shropshire Way (SW) across country through the scattered community of Whixall and on to Hollingwood, a small village about 1 mile from the border with Wales. It then continues north on the original Shropshire Way route, before heading to Blackoe Bridge, for a relaxing 2½ mile return alongside the canal. Allow about 4 hours

START Roundthorne Bridge, Whixall Moss [SJ 501357].

DIRECTIONS From the A495, 3 miles west of Whitchurch, take a road south signposted to Fenns Bank/Whixall/Fenns Moss NNR. At the junction in Fenn's Bank follow the road ahead south past a side road, then at a T-junction turn left across a bridge over the canal at Platt Lane. Immediately turn right along a narrow road, signposted 'Canal Side', beside the canal, later bending across Roundthorne Bridge 44 over the canal to a junction of tracks. Turn right to a nearby small canalside parking area by information boards on the Mosses Trails.

1 Cross bridge 44 over the canal and go through a kissing gate ahead. Follow the signposted kissing gated SW across two fields, then along the next field edge, through a hedge gap in the corner and on across the fourth field to a road. Follow it LEFT past Whixall Primary School and a side road. At the next junction turn RIGHT signposted to Bostock Hall/Wem. Shortly, take the signposted SW over a stile on the left and across the field to go through a gate in its right-hand corner. Just beyond go half-LEFT between large trees up to join the large field boundary on your right. Follow it past a small pool to go through a waymarked SW gate in its top corner at a junction of two sections of the Shropshire Way Turn LEFT to cross a nearby stile/sleeper bridge/stile.

2 Turn RIGHT along the field edge to a sleeper bridge/stile in the corner. Go

half-LEFT across the field to pass between an old tree and a possibly dried up pond, then on towards Millhouse Cottage and past its garden hedge corner to a gate. Follow its driveway shared with nearby Millhouse Farm to a road. Take the signposted SW through a gate opposite and down the middle of the field towards a farm then cross a stile by a gate in the boundary on the left. Follow the path to a stile and on to another. Go past the large oak tree ahead to a further stile and on to a hidden gate in the hedge onto a road. Follow it north past Cumberland Lane and houses in Hollingwood. At the T-junction turn LEFT, signposted Platt Lane/ Whixall. As the road bends half-left turn RIGHT on the original SW along Mossey House Farm's access track.

3 After a few yards go through a way-marked bridleway/SW small gate on the right. Go up the edge of the large field past the very large outbuildings to a waymarked gate in the top field corner. Go up the next very long field to a small gate in the right-hand corner. Follow the gated bridleway along the next field edge to a road. Follow the stony track opposite along the large field, shortly bending left to go through a gateway and ending. Go up the edge of the next large field towards Fields Farm and through a gateway in the corner. Go along the field edge to a stile in the corner and down the next field edge past a stile round to another by an old gate. Go briefly along the next field edge, then turn RIGHT to a waymarked stile/ gate and go along the wide hedge-lined path to the farm. Continue along its driveway past houses to a road. Follow it LEFT, soon descending.

4 At a sign for Fenns Meadow Green Burial Ground, cross a stile by a gate on the right. Follow the waymarked byway up the field edge to a stile/gate by Scots pines. Continue along the waymarked byway, then cross a stile on the left and one ahead. Go along the field edge past burials to a stile in the corner. Go down the middle of the large field towards a telegraph pole at the bottom to a stile 15 yards to its right. Go half-RIGHT down the field to a stile/footbridge in the tree boundary. Go half-LEFT across the next field up to stile in another tree boundary. Descend to cross a stream and a stile above. Go across the next field to a telegraph pole – *with the canal just below* – then bear RIGHT to a stile onto a road.

5 Turn LEFT across Blackoe Bridge no. 40 over the canal and continue briefly down the road then do a sharp U-turn along a track on the right back to the canal. Go under the bridge and continue southwards on the towpath along the mature tree-lined canal. After passing under bridge 43 at Platt Lane the canal continues along a long open section. When the towpath ends join the bend of a nearby stony access track and follow it beside the canal to the start.

Roundthorne Bridge, 44

WALK 30

GRINDLEY BROOK

DESCRIPTION This 4½ mile walk follows the short restored section of the Whitchurch Branch Canal, then the main canal to Grindley Brook, with its famous staircase locks, café and pub refreshments. It then returns across fields to the canal to reach the canal junction. After a short extension to Whitchurch Wharf (optional), it follows popular local paths then returns through the Waterways Country Park. Allow about 2½ hrs.

START Waterways Country Park car park [SJ 532415].

DIRECTIONS From the A41/A525 roundabout at Whitchurch follow the Country Park signs along the B5398, then left along Chemistry and left again at a mini-roundabout along Meadowcroft to find the nearby car park on the right.

*T*he main canal, completed in 1805, bypassed Whitchurch, but with financial support from local businessmen, a branch into the town was built and opened in 1811. New industries, including a gasworks, silk mill and corn mill were established by the canal, and Whitchurch prospered. Commercial traffic continued until 1936. The branch closed in 1944 and was partly built over. A short section was restored in 1993 and there are plans to extend into a new canal basin.

I Follow a path down into the Country Park, then turn LEFT along another path under the road bridge then the

one remaining traditional bridge of the former Whitchurch Branch Canal. Now follow the restored canal, privately owned by Whitchurch Waterways Trust, to its junction with the main Llangollen Canal. Cross lift bridge 31 and turn RIGHT along the towpath – *now on the Sandstone Trail and a spur of the new Shropshire Way*. Follow the canal to Grindley Brook Wharf and its staircase

locks. *Note the former lock-keepers cottage, with its curved bay window. Opposite was once a mill.* Descend alongside the locks to Lock Café and under A49 bridge 29, then past three further locks to leave the canal at bridge 28. Follow a stony lane past houses to the A49. Cross to the Horse and Jockey pub opposite.

2 Cross the adjoining B5395 and go along the pavement beside the A49. Shortly turn RIGHT along Bubney Farm's driveway.

32

On its bend go past a tree ahead to a stile/gate, then along the field edge to another stile/gate. Go along the field edge to a gate and the next field near a farm track, then turn LEFT across a stile, farm track and stile opposite. Go across two fields to bridge 30 over the canal, then follow it back to its junction. After continuing along the canal to Whitchurch Wharf return to cross lift bridge 31 and turn LEFT along the canal to a kissing gate.

3 Follow a wide path up the field, soon taking its left fork to a tree boundary. Take the path's right fork up to go through a small gate at a waymarked path junction. Follow the path down to a kissing gate, then across the next field to another. Descend through trees, turn LEFT along a path, then RIGHT between houses, over a road and down to a wide stony cross-path. Follow it RIGHT through Waterways Country Park to an information board. Take the left fork to a road. Angle LEFT across it and turn RIGHT along a signposted stony path to the start.

WALK 31

WIRSWALL

DESCRIPTION An undulating 4½ mile walk, featuring three popular recreation trails, a section of the canal, and two interesting pubs. The route first follows the Sandstone Trail along the Llangollen Canal to Willymoor Lock Tavern, then the initial section of Bishop Bennet's Way (BBW) up to Wirswall. Here the BBW joins the South Cheshire Way for a descent in stages back to Grindley Brook. Allow about 2½ hours.

START Horse and Jockey car park, Grindley Brook [SJ 522432].

DIRECTIONS The Horse and Jockey pub lies at the A41/B5395 junction in Grindley Brook, just to the north west of Whitchurch. Parking, preferably near the pub entrance, is allowed but please take refreshments in return.

1 From the car park entrance cross with care the A41 to the garage entrance opposite and follow a signposted bridleway/BBW along a stony lane. At bridge 28 over the canal turn LEFT down to the towpath and follow the canal under nearby former railway bridge 27 and on through open countryside. Later you pass Povey's lock then reach Willymoor Lock Tavern – *once the lock-keeper's cottage and now a delightful canalside pub.* After refreshments cross the footbridge over the canal to the car park. Turn RIGHT by the fence, then RIGHT across a stream, alongside the race, then back over the stream to a stile. Follow a track to a stile on its bend onto the A49. Turn RIGHT along the verge then LEFT up Bradley Green Lane opposite. When it becomes two stony access tracks follow the one ahead, then continue up a tree/hedge lined bridleway and through trees to a gate. Go up the hedge-lined green track ahead, then continue up the now sunken tree-lined track. Shortly turn LEFT through a gate and up a short green track to join a stony track. Follow it to the road in Wirswall by an information board on the BBW. Turn RIGHT.

2 Follow the road down through the village. After just over ⅓ mile, immediately before The Bungalow, turn RIGHT along a hedge/tree lined bridleway to a stile/gate. Follow the bridleway ahead below the fence down to a gate, then alongside the tree boundary and on past Hinton Old Hall. Follow its driveway to the A49. Cross it with care to follow the access track opposite to Hinton Bank Farm. Go past the house and continue ahead past nearby Hinton Villa. Before the track bends right to Hinton Manor, turn LEFT down the short adjoining field edge to a facing gate by a water trough. Just beyond turn RIGHT down a tree-lined green track. When it bends left into a field continue ahead down a delightful, initially sunken, old green track, soon levelling out. At a farm track go through a waymarked gate opposite. Go up the faint green bridleway ahead and continue beside the boundary to a gate in the corner. Go along the next field edge to a small gate/stile near a farm. Go half-RIGHT across the field to follow the fence alongside the farm's access track to a gate in the corner onto the track. Follow it under the old railway bridge and across the canal to join your outward route.

WALK 32

BIG MERE

DESCRIPTION A 6 mile undulating walk of great variety from the attractive Cheshire village of Marbury, with a canalside pub midway and one to finish. After visiting St Michael's church, the route follows the waymarked South Cheshire Way (SCW) past the wooded side of Big Mere, then rises across low hills, offering extensive views, to Wicksted Old Hall and Wirswall. After following the Bishop Bennet Way down a delightful bridleway and lane to the A49, it joins the Llangollen Canal at Willymoor Lock Tavern. The route returns along the canal then field paths to Marbury. Allow about 3½ hours.

START Village green, Marbury [SJ 561457].

DIRECTIONS Marbury lies about 3 miles north of Whitchurch. The small village green, containing a 200 year old oak tree, lies at the road junction by the Swan Inn. There is roadside parking on Wrenbury Road beyond the pub.

Marbury, dating from Anglo-Saxon times, lies next to two meres, glacial lakes formed at the end of the last Ice Age. At its heart is the Swan Inn, an hostelry since the mid 18thC, attractive timber-framed buildings and St Michael's church overlooking the Big Mere, a popular fishing lake. The red sandstone church, built in the 16thC on the site of an earlier church, contains a 15thC wooden pulpit, the oldest in Cheshire. Its six bells were hung in 1799 and rehung in 1928. The arrival of the canal near the village provided a transport route for local cheesemaking farms.

I At the junction turn RIGHT up Wirswall road then LEFT along a lane to St Michael's church and a good view of Big Mere. Return to the junction and continue along Hollins Lane past cottages then take a signposted path through a gate on the right, now on the SCW. Go across the field to a stile at the corner of Big Mere. Follow the path past the side of the lake to a stile/gate and on past woodland to another near the lake's next corner. Follow the path along the field by the wood to a stile/gate. Just beyond bear LEFT with the wood up the edge of the field, passing close to the wood corner, then continue with the path up the field, soon joining a faint green track.

2 Just beyond a solitary tree on your right and before the top wood corner bear RIGHT up the slope beneath a small ridge. After levelling out angle LEFT past the end of the ridge to a stile/gate in the boundary corner. Go along the edge of the large field to stiles in the corner, then up the middle of the next field to a stile/gate in its top left-hand corner – *a good place to stop to enjoy the extensive views.* Go up the large field to a stile in a wooden fence and across the next field to a stile by a finger post. Don't cross it but turn RIGHT with the SCW along the field edge to a stile/gate. Continue ahead along a stony track to pass through 19thC Wicksted Old Hall, soon bending right along its gravel driveway to a road. Follow it LEFT into Wirswall.

3 Just before it bends left at an information board on the Bishop Benett Way, turn RIGHT along the stony hedge-lined track, soon bending left past woodland. At its end by Six Acres continue down a short narrow green track to a gate at a fingerpost. Just beyond turn RIGHT down a sunken tree-lined earth track, then continue with the hedge-lined track. When it bends right into a field go through a gate ahead. Follow the predominantly tree-lined bridleway down to a stony access track from a nearby house, then continue down narrow Bradley Green Lane to the A49. Cross with care and turn RIGHT along the verge to a nearby stile. Go along a track to a stile just before the canal, over a stream, alongside the race, and into the car park. Cross a footbridge over the canal lock by Willymoor Lock Tavern – *once the lock-keeper's cottage and now a delightful canalside pub.*

4 After refreshments follow the towpath northwards along the attractive canal. After passing Quoisley Lock, the canal runs close to the A49 before passing under it

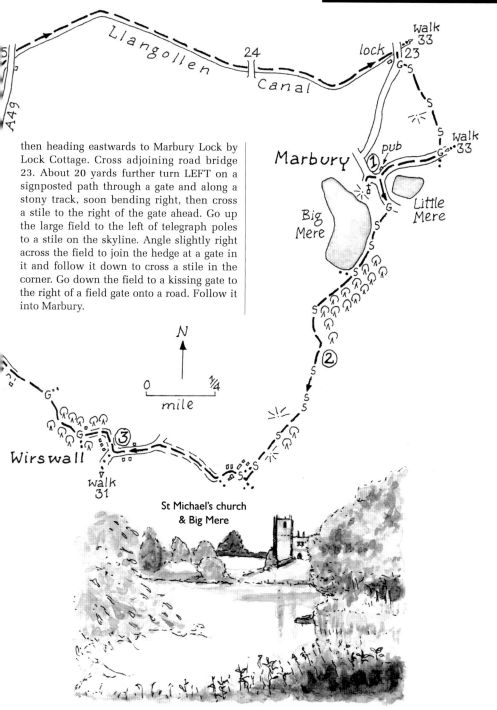

then heading eastwards to Marbury Lock by Lock Cottage. Cross adjoining road bridge 23. About 20 yards further turn LEFT on a signposted path through a gate and along a stony track, soon bending right, then cross a stile to the right of the gate ahead. Go up the large field to the left of telegraph poles to a stile on the skyline. Angle slightly right across the field to join the hedge at a gate in it and follow it down to cross a stile in the corner. Go down the field to a kissing gate to the right of a field gate onto a road. Follow it into Marbury.

St Michael's church & Big Mere

WRENBURY & MARBURY

DESCRIPTION A 7¼ mile walk exploring the countryside between the attractive Cheshire villages of Wrenbury and Marbury. The route follows the waymarked South Cheshire Way (SCW) to Marbury, with its 18thC inn, 16thC church, and two meres (for more information see Walk 32), then returns along the canal to Wrenbury and a choice of two pubs. Allow about 4 hours.

START Recreation Ground car park, Wrenbury [SJ 596476].

DIRECTIONS Wrenbury is best reached from the A49 by the Cholmondeley Arms. After crossing the canal and entering the village continue past the church and Village Stores, then at Wrenbury Medical Centre turn left into the large car park.

*W*renbury, *an ancient settlement recorded in the Domesday book in 1086, stands on the Llangollen Canal and Crewe-Shrewsbury railway line. It was included in the lands donated to the Cistercian Combermere Abbey around 1180, but after the Dissolution in 1539, became under the auspices of Cotton family for centuries. The red sandstone early 16thC St Margaret's Church, overlooking the village green, includes a rare example of a dog whipper's pew and a memorial to Stapleton Cotton. In the churchyard is a small black-and-white 17thC cottage, reputedly a former almshouse and school. The section of the Llangollen Canal near the village has three rare single-span timber lift bridges dating from the 1790s, which are among Thomas Telford's earliest works. They were designed to be operated manually using counterbalancing beam weights. Wrenbury road bridge no. 20 is now operated by a modern power winch.*

I From the car park entrance turn LEFT along the pavement. After passing the late Victorian Primary School, with its bell-cote and weathervane, cross the road and

follow the pavement along Station Road. After crossing a stream, the pavement continues opposite. Just before the level crossing at Wrenbury Station cross to a stony track opposite, then take the signposted path through a small gate on the right. *You are now on a section of the South Cheshire Way.* Follow the path across two fields, later passing just to the right of a solitary tree to a stile in the hedge/tree boundary ahead. Follow the path through the next field to a stile in the corner, then along another field edge to a gate onto a road opposite the driveway to Smeaton Hall. Turn RIGHT along the road, then cross a stile on the left. Go slightly LEFT across the field to a waymark post and on past a small pond, bending left to a stile/gate at the garden corner of nearby Smeaton Hall.

2 Continue ahead to another stile and along a short fenced track leading from the farm. Go through a waymarked gate and along the field edge, in the corner bending left to a nearby stile/footbridge/stile. The path now angles RIGHT across the field to a stile/gate at the end of farm outbuildings. Go along the edge of the next field to cross a stile on the left, then go half-RIGHT through the edge of trees to a stile at the corner of a small wood and another beyond into a field. Turn LEFT to a nearby stile in the corner, then RIGHT along the edge of the next field to a stile/small gate in the corner. Continue

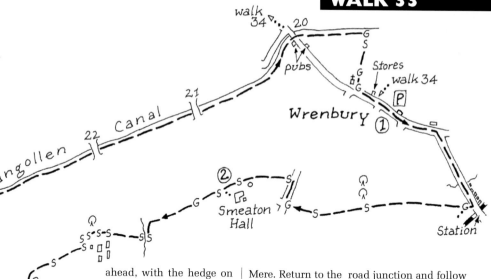

ahead, with the hedge on your left, to a waymarked fence corner by a small pond. Continue along a green track between fields, then along a concrete farm track and through a gate by an information board about 'Riches in Ditches'.

3 At the corner of the fence on your right turn RIGHT on the waymarked SCW, then head half-LEFT up the field to the left of a line of telegraph poles, over the concrete farm track and on up the field edge to a small metal gate. Cross a stile ahead onto a stony access track from a nearby Hurst Hall. Follow it LEFT then turn RIGHT along a road. Just before the first large house on the right in Marbury go through a kissing gate on the left into a field. Follow the boundary on the right to a kissing gate in the corner. Go between the house and outbuildings, then along its stony access track. *Hidden to the right is Little Mere.* At the road turn RIGHT – *with a view of Big Mere and prominent St Michael's church* – to the junction by the *18thC Swan Inn and the magnificent 200 year old oak tree encircled by a seat.*

4 Before starting the return journey first go up Wirswall road between timber-framed buildings, then turn LEFT along a lane to St. Michael's church. Follow the path round to its entrance and a good view of Big Mere. Return to the road junction and follow Wrenbury Road past the Swan Inn through the village to meet your outward route. Here go through a kissing gate on the left and up the field to a stile in the right hand corner. Turn LEFT up the next field edge beside the hedge, then at a gate in it angle RIGHT gradually across the field to a part-hidden stile in the boundary ahead. Go down the large field to the right of telegraph poles to a stile. Just beyond turn LEFT along a track to a gate onto a road. Follow it RIGHT over a watercourse to bridge 23 over the Llangollen Canal by Lock Cottage and Marbury Lock. Turn RIGHT down to the wide grass towpath.

5 Follow it eastwards for 2 miles to lift bridge 20 by the Dusty Miller pub – *a former mid 18thC corn mill* – at the road in Wrenbury. *Just down the road is The Cotton Arms, a traditional country pub.* Cross the road and continue along the towpath past Wrenbury Mill basin. The attractive former grain store building forms part of the marine services site, which includes a dry dock and boat repair/hire facilities. At lift bridge 19 turn RIGHT to a kissing gate and follow the path to a stile and across the field to a kissing gate. Follow the stony path through St Margaret's churchyard to the road in Wrenbury. Turn LEFT along the pavement past the Village Stores/PO to the start.

WALK 34

BADDILEY

DESCRIPTION A 6½ mile walk from Wrenbury (See Walk 33 for information) through the attractive ancient manor of Baddiley in South Cheshire. After visiting ancient St.Margaret's church, the route enjoys a short section of canal to Wrenbury Mill basin and two interesting pubs. It then follows field paths across a low ridge, before passing through the scattered settlement of Baddiley, featuring natural and man made lakes, fine red-bricked farms, and the ancient timber-framed St Michael's church (open to visitors every Saturday, April-October, 10-4) by Baddiley Hall. It then returns along the canal. Allow about 3½ hours.

START Recreational Ground car park, Wrenbury [SJ 596476].

DIRECTIONS See Walk 33.

From the car park entrance turn RIGHT along the pavement past the Village Stores/PO then go into St Margaret's churchyard. Follow the path past the end of the church to a kissing gate, then another path across the field to a stile and on to a kissing gate to join the Llangollen Canal by lift bridge 19. Turn LEFT along the towpath past moored boats to lift bridge 20 at Wrenbury Mill basin. *The attractive former grain store building forms part of the marine services site, which includes a dry dock and boat repair/hire facilities. Nearby is the Dusty Miller pub, a former mid 18thC corn mill, and just down the road is the traditional Cotton Arms.* Cross the bridge and go along the road ahead, then take a side road angling up on the right. On the bend go through a kissing gate ahead and along the edge of two fields, then follow the waymarked path through the edge of mature woodland. Go past a stile at its corner and along the tree-lined path to a gate. Continue along the edge of the next field to a stile/gate, then a larger one to a small gate in the corner.

2 Just beyond turn RIGHT along the field edge and down to a gate. Angle RIGHT

from the farm track to a stile/gate, then follow the hedge on your right up the field to cross a footbridge and stile just before the corner. Go ahead across the field, soon joining the hedge/tree boundary on your right to a waymarked step-over fence in the corner. Continue through vegetation then along the field edge. With a view ahead of Baddiley Reservoir, go half-LEFT to a stile in the tree boundary ahead. Go along the edge of the next field past a stile and on – *with a view of Baddiley Mere* – to a stile/gate in the corner. Go along the next field edge past a nearby pool and through a facing gate in the corner. Just beyond go through a waymarked gate on the right. Go up and across the middle of the large field to cross a stile in its far left corner to the unexpected sight of another lake. Go half-RIGHT to an old waymarked gatepost – *with a good view along Baddiley Mere* – then turn LEFT passing to the right of a clump of trees to a stile ahead. Go along the field edge – *with a view of nearby Dairy House Farm* – to cross a stile in the corner and one beyond. Turn LEFT up the field edge to stiles onto Dairy House Farm's driveway (a bridleway). Follow it RIGHT – *with a view of St Michael's church* – to a stony cross track by a farm. Follow it RIGHT between the single storey dwelling and a small pool and on to visit the church. *This unusual church dates from at least 1308 and is said to be one of the oldest timber-framed churches in Europe. Nearby is Baddiley Hall, dating from the 18thC on the site of an earlier manor house.*

3 Return along the track to the single-storey farm complex, then at its garden corner turn RIGHT along its perimeter to a small gate and a kissing gate beyond. Follow the path to another kissing gate and straight ahead across the field to cross stiled bridge 13 over the Llangollen Canal, then turn LEFT to a stile onto the towpath. Go under the bridge and continue along

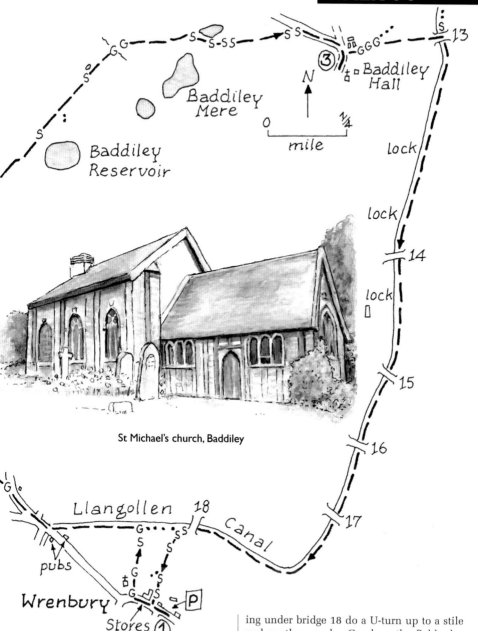

St Michael's church, Baddiley

Llangollen 18 Canal

pubs

Wrenbury

Stores ①

the towpath past Baddiley locks 3 and 2, under bridge 14 and past lock 1. *Nearby is the attractive 17thC timber-framed Starkeys Farm.* Continue along the canal. After pass- ing under bridge 18 do a U-turn up to a stile and another nearby. Go along the field edge to a stile and along the next field edge past a stile to a stile on the left at its end. Follow a hedged/tree lined green track to the road by the Village Stores. Turn LEFT back to the start.

HURLESTON JUNCTION

DESCRIPTION A 5 mile walk from an attractive Cheshire village featuring two canals. The route heads west across fields to Swanley, then follows the final section of the Llangollen Canal for just over 2 miles to Hurleston Junction, before returning along a ½ mile section of the main Shropshire Union Canal. Allow about 2½ hours.

START Car park, Acton [SJ 633530].

DIRECTIONS Acton village lies on the A534 just west of Nantwich. The car park is on the eastern side of the road between the church and the Star pub.

*A*cton *is mentioned in the Doomsday Book of 1086. St Mary's church, dating from the 12thC, stands on the site of an earlier Saxon church. Its tower is said to be the oldest in Cheshire. In the churchyard is a tall 17thC sundial, converted from a medieval cross, and two 17thC almshouses. The church was used by the Royalists during the Civil War Battle of Nantwich in 1644 – a key victory for Parliamentarians.*

I From the car park entrance cross the road and turn LEFT along the pavement opposite past the Star pub, then take a footpath signposted to Marsh Lane along a wide stony track. Soon, at a waymarked junction of paths. turn RIGHT. Follow a path across three fields, then through trees and along a house's stony access track to a road. Take a signposted path opposite across two fields to another road. Cross a stile opposite, then angle RIGHT across the field to a stile in the corner onto a road. Follow it LEFT to a junction at Swanley village. Follow the road ahead to a nearby bridge over the Llangollen Canal, where you join the towpath.

2 Follow the canal northwards, past Swanley Locks and Swanley Bridge Marina, then under bridges, later passing Bachehouse Pool and 17thC Bache House

beyond. As you approach Hurleston Locks, you have a view of nearby Hurleston reservoir – *originally built to supply water, extracted from the river Dee at Llantysilio and carried by the Llangollen Canal, to the main Shropshire Union Canal, it is now also used for domestic drinking water. This vital feeder role saved the Llangollen branch from closure.* Follow the series of locks down to Hurleston Junction, then cross bridge 97 over the Shropshire Union Canal.

3 Follow the canal southwards then cross bridge 93 – *with an information board on the Battle of Nantwich, which took place nearby.* After a small gate follow the path up the field to another gate. Follow the hedge-lined path then track between houses to a nearby estate road in Acton. Follow it RIGHT to the main road. Turn LEFT past the church to the start.

WELSH FRANKTON TO QUEEN'S HEAD

DESCRIPTION A 5¼ mile linear walk combining sections of the Llangollen and Montgomery Canals, featuring two canalside pubs. Allow about 2½ hours.

START Narrowboat Inn, Welsh Frankton [SJ 353325].

Park opposite the Queen's Head pub (See Walk 38) and take the frequent 70 bus to Oswestry, then take the 449 to the Narrowboat Inn, Welsh Frankton on the A495. Follow the Llangollen Canal to Lower Frankton, then the Montgomery Canal to Queen's Head.

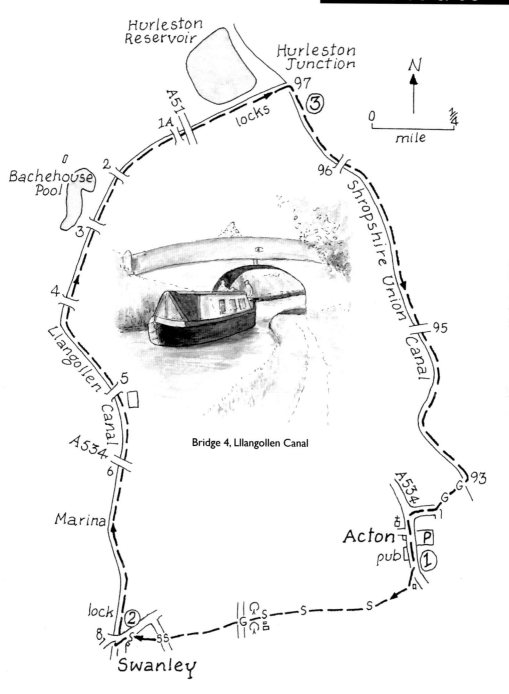

Bridge 4, Lllangollen Canal

Hurleston Reservoir

Hurleston Junction

97

3

N

0 ¼ mile

A51

1A

locks

2

Bachehouse Pool

3

96

Shropshire Union Canal

95

4

Llangollen Canal

5

A534

6

93

A534 G-G

Marina

Acton
pub 1
P

lock 2

8

SS

S - - S - - - S

Swanley

WALK 37

ST WINIFRED'S WELL

DESCRIPTION A 6 mile (**A**) or 5½ mile (**B**) walk featuring a section of the scenic Montgomery Canal, an ancient healing well, two canalside pubs, and a tea-room. The route passes through Oswestry Golf Course then continues to Maesbury Marsh, once a busy inland port supplying Oswestry. Walk B goes direct to the 18thC Navigation Inn, while Walk A first extends to the Canal Centre tea-room. After a short diversion to St Winifred's Well the route returns along the canal. Allow about 3½ hours. For information on the canal see Walk 18.)

START Queen's Head [SJ 339268].

DIRECTIONS Queen's Head lies just off the A5 by the Montgomery Canal, about 3 miles from Oswestry. There is a small public canalside car park opposite the Queen's Head pub below its own additional car park, and alternative parking on the nearby side road. Arriva bus 70 (Oswestry-Shrewsbury) also stops here frequently.

1 From the pub follow the pavement up to cross the B5009, then bend RIGHT along the busy A5 and cross it with care to Oswestry Golf Club opposite. Angle RIGHT through the car park to the Clubhouse corner. Continue in the same direction down the tree-covered golf course to a blue waymark post amongst trees. Follow the waymarked path past golf tees to more trees, where it angles right up to a low walled sunken section, then descends to a stiled footbridge at the course perimeter. Go across the field to a stile, then across a green track and through the wood, then a narrow field to a stile. Go half-LEFT, then continue up the field – *with a view of 18thC Aston Hall* – to a kissing gate in its left-hand corner. Follow the fence on your left to a gate, with Keeper's Cottage nearby.

2 Follow the line of old trees along the edge of two fields, go through an old tree boundary and continue along a large field

edge past Fox Hall Farm to a stile just before the corner. Go along the farm's driveway to a nearby road. Follow it ahead to Bromwich Park. *Here are the remains of a medieval moated site and formal gardens.* Continue along a stony track, later taking its right fork. It then becomes Waen Lane which leads to a junction in Maesbury Marsh. (For Walk B turn left.) Turn RIGHT along the pavement opposite, then LEFT along Coed y Rae to cross the bridge over the canal by the Canal Centre. Follow the canal eastwards to bridge 79 by the Navigation Inn, which predates the canal. *The remains of an old crane stands on the former 18thC canal wharf. An information board tells its history. There was once a smelting house and bone manure works here.*

3 Continue along the narrow canal. At bridge 78, to visit St Winifred's Well, go up to the nearby gate, then slightly left across the large field to a stile in its corner. Go along the next field edge to a kissing gate and

footbridge beyond to a small timber-framed building, below which is the well. *Dedicated to 7thC St Winifred, it is on the site of a spring which reputedly flowed after her bones were rested here in the 12thC whilst being taken from the more famous shrine in Holywell in North Wales to Shrewsbury. Its miraculous healing properties have attracted pilgrims for centuries. The innermost of the three pools is the medieval well chamber and the building is the medieval well chapel, later used as a court house and now a Landmark Trust holiday cottage.* Return to the canal. Follow it past Aston Locks and a house, then after passing under bridge 76A follow the track up to the road junction in Queen's Head.

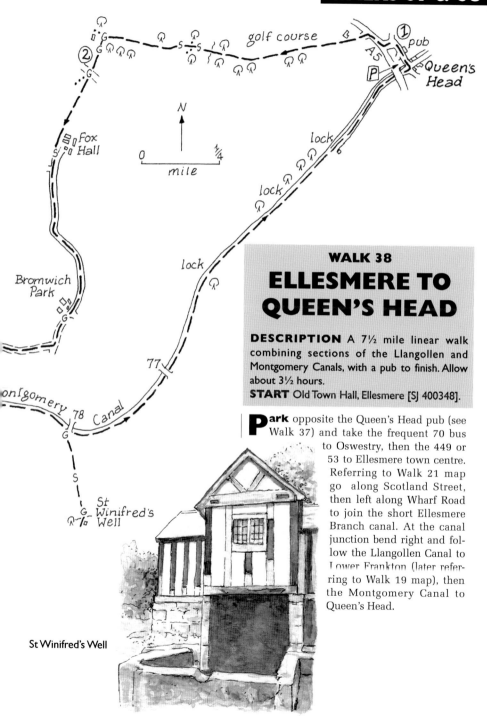

WALK 38

ELLESMERE TO QUEEN'S HEAD

DESCRIPTION A 7½ mile linear walk combining sections of the Llangollen and Montgomery Canals, with a pub to finish. Allow about 3½ hours.

START Old Town Hall, Ellesmere [SJ 400348].

Park opposite the Queen's Head pub (see Walk 37) and take the frequent 70 bus to Oswestry, then the 449 or 53 to Ellesmere town centre. Referring to Walk 21 map go along Scotland Street, then left along Wharf Road to join the short Ellesmere Branch canal. At the canal junction bend right and follow the Llangollen Canal to Lower Frankton (later referring to Walk 19 map), then the Montgomery Canal to Queen's Head.

St Winifred's Well

43

PRONUNCIATION

Welsh	English equivalent
c	always hard, as in **c**at
ch	as in the Scottish word lo**ch**
dd	as th in **th**en
f	as f in o**f**
ff	as ff in o**ff**
g	always hard as in **g**ot
ll	no real equivalent. It is like 'th' in then, but with an 'L' sound added to it, giving 'thlan' for the pronunciation of the Welsh 'Llan'.

In Welsh the accent usually falls on the last-but-one syllable of a word.

KEY TO THE MAPS

- ➡ Walk route and direction
- ═══ Metalled road
- ─ ─ ─ Unsurfaced road
- • • • • Footpath/route adjoining walk route
- ～～➔ River/stream
- ♣ ۞ Trees
- ▬■▬ Railway
- **G** Gate
- **S** Stile
- **F.B.** Footbridge
- ⩊⃥ Viewpoint
- **P** Parking
- **T** Telephone

THE COUNTRYSIDE CODE

- Be safe – plan ahead and follow any signs
- Leave gates and property as you find them
- Protect plants and animals, and take your litter home
- Keep dogs under close control
- Consider other people

The routes follow public rights of way or permissive paths. Please report any Rights of Way problems online to the relevant Rights of Way section of Denbighire County Council, Wrexham County Borough Council, Shropshire Council or Cheshire East Council.Each walk has a detailed map and description but please be aware that changes in detail can occur at any time.

About the author

David is an experienced walker with a love of the countryside and an interest in local history, including canals. He is the author of a series of walks guidebooks covering North Wales, where he has lived and worked for many years. He has worked as a Rights of Way surveyor across North Wales, been a freelance writer for Walking Wales magazine, and served as a member of Denbighshire Local Access Forum.

Whether on a riverside ramble, mountain or long distance walk, he greatly appreciates the beauty, culture and history of the landscape and hopes that his comprehensive guidebooks will encourage people to explore on foot its diverse scenery and rich heritage. For more information visit www.davidberrywalks.co.uk

Published by **Kittiwake-Books Limited**
3 Glantwymyn Village Workshops, Glantwymyn, Machynlleth, Montgomeryshire SY20 8LY

© Text & map research: David Berry 2016
© Maps & illustrations: Kittiwake-Books Ltd 2016
Drawings by Morag Perrott
Cover photos: Main: Lift bridge near Whitchurch.
Inset: Chirk Aqueduct. David Berry.

Care has been taken to be accurate. However neither the author nor the publisher can accept responsibility for any errors which may appear, or their consequences. If you are in any doubt about access, check before you proceed.

Printed by Mixam UK.

ISBN: **978 1 908748 34 8**